GOLD AND SILVER EMBROIDERY

Edited by Kit Pyman

SEARCH PRESS

"You don't need special eyes...

...to s̶p̶e̶c̶i̶a̶l̶i̶s̶e̶ specialise"

MADEIRA

GOLD AND SILVER EMBROIDERY

Madeira is a leading manufacturer of high quality machine embroidery thread and specialist threads for handicrafts. Used throughout the world for many years, Madeira's extensive product range includes:

Six Strand Cotton in 324 stunning colours produced from top quality long staple Egyptian cotton, double mercerise and fast dyed to 95°C in innovative spiral packaging containing 25% more thread than a standard 8 metre skein.

'Tanne' machine embroidery cotton, manufactured to the same high quality a Madeira's Six Strand, is available in 170 colours in six different counts: 80s, 50s, 30s, 20s, and 12s.
'Tanne' is also used for lacemaking, quilting, crocheting, etc.

Rayon No. 40 manufactured from 100% Viscose, is the premier high quality machine embroidery thread, proven by industry throughout the world for over 30 years.

Neon No. 40 will give you a strikingly different effect: available in a range of shocking fluorescent and plain colours and manufactured from 100% filament Polyester.

Metallic No. 40 for use as a needle or bobbin thread and is available in 30 rich colours and opalescent shades.

Toledo is ideal for monogramming and decorative top stitching. It is the finest count machine embroidery thread manufactured from 100% Viscose in a b 60 colour range.

Machine Sewing Thread No. 15 is a strong, true 3 ply sewing thread used on high speed sewing machines, perfect for seaming.

Metallic Thread No. 5 is supplied in Madeira's special 20 metre spiral packs in 5 antique colours of gold and silver, ideal for a wide range of church embroidery, restoration work and many other craft uses.

Decor is used for hand and machine embroidery as well as a knitting accompanying yarn where it adds a soft, high lustre look to the finished garment, endless possibilities in 36 shimmering colours.

Metallic Thread No. 3 in 4 bright shades of silver and gold and is available in 20 metre spiral packs. It's ideal for use as a couched thread, church embroidery, cord, tassel and braid making, etc.

Burmilana Nos. 3 and 12 manufactured from 70% Acrylic and 30% wool, the rich texture of Burmilana is available in a wide range of shades for machine embroidery, lacemaking and other craft uses.

Madeira No. 40 the premier viscose machine embroidery thread with high lustre available in 240 mouthwatering colours, used throughout the world for decorative purposes by industry.

Sticku No. 30 is a thicker 100% Viscose thread than Madeira No. 40, achieving greater coverage for a lower number of stitches in 110 eyecatching colours.

Metallised Yarn No. 120 gives glamorous sparkle when used as an accompanying yarn in a knitted garment. As with all Madeira's knitting accompanying yarns, No. 120 can be used for either hand or machine knitting.

Metallised Yarn No. 50 adds an opalescent pearl-like high-priced appearance to knitted garments.

Knitting-in Elastic is manufactured in translucent light and dark shades, so it's virtually invisible in the garment. Madeira knitting-in elastic is essential with many modern, fancy and cotton yarns to keep your garment in shape.

Metallised Yarn No. 10 can be used as a knitting accompanying yarn or on its own, either way with excitingly different results. Additionally, No. 10 is used for hand embroidery, lacemaking, crocheting, tatting, pin art etc.

MADEIRA

Madeira with its headquarters located in the beautiful Black Forest region of West Germany was formed some 70 years ago and is now in the hands of the third generation of the founding family. Madeira is the specialist manufacturer of high quality embroidery and decorative threads upon which Madeira's international reputation has been built.

Madeira machine embroidery threads are tested for use on all known domestic embroidery and sewing machines as well as on all types of modern automatic machines, with over 30 product ranges available and the widest selection of colour to enable the company to meet the demands of the fashion and handicrafts industries.

Madeira specially developed 100% Viscose Rayon threads for use on embroidery machines over thirty years ago and continue a policy of new product development: working in close harmony with manufacturers, fashion designers and those involved in the use of decorative thread throughout the world. The technical production of threads extends to the close co-operation with manufacturers of associated machinery for the efficient production of the highest quality threads. Madeira guarantees the quality of its products: they are the ultimate in runnability with exacting production standards to ensure the quality which is their business.

When it comes to creativity, when it comes to inspiration and when it comes to quality, make sure you insist on Madeira, for the most exciting specialist craft threads available.

First published 1987 by Search Press Ltd, Wellwood, North Farm Road, Tunbridge Wells, Kent TN2 3DR

Text by Valerie Campbell-Harding, Joan Cleaver, Pat Phillpott, Jane Lemon and Jane Dew. Drawings by Jan Messent. Editor: Kit Pyman Designer: David Stanley Photographs by Search Press Studios.

Cover. The embroidered lettering on the front of the cover is worked by Jackey Hill.

ISBN 0 85532 588 7

For your nearest stockist contact **Madeira Threads (U.K.) Ltd.,** Ryder House, Back Lane, Boroughbridge, N. Yorkshire, YO5 9AT. Tel: 09012 3555 Telex: 57944 Madira G Fax: 09012 4176
Madeira (U.S.A.) Ltd., 56 Primrose Drive, O'Shea Industrial Park, Laconia, New Hampshire 03246 U.S.A. Tel: 603 528 2944 Toll-free 1 800 225 3001 Telex: 753581 Madeira UD Fax: 603 528 4264
Madeira Garnfabrik Rudolf Schmidt KG, Zinkmattenstrasse 38, Postfach 320,D7800 Freiburg, W. Germany. Tel: (0761) 55081/82 Telex: 772622 MAGA D Fax: (0761) 508456

Contents

List of Contributors   6

Chapter 1.   INTRODUCTION: History of metal-thread work   7
by Kit Pyman

Chapter 2.   GOLDWORK: Techniques of metal-thread   15
embroidery *by Valerie Campbell-Harding*

Chapter 3.   APPLIQUÉ: Technique and hand appliqué   41
by Joan Cleaver

Machine and detached appliqué
by Pat Phillpott

Chapter 4.   MACHINE EMBROIDERY: WITH METALLIC   53
THREADS *by Pat Phillpott*

Chapter 5.   LETTERING *by Pat Phillpott*   75

Chapter 6.   CHURCH EMBROIDERY *by Jane Lemon*   83

Chapter 7.   BEADWORK AND TAMBOUR BEADING   93
by Jane Dew

SEQUINS, JEWELS, GLASS AND STONES
by Valerie Campbell-Harding

Index   112

Useful Addresses   112

List of contributors

Kathryn Biggam

Allison Blair

Christine Bolland

Valerie Campbell-Harding

Jean Brown

Jane Clarke

Joan Cleaver

Mollie Collins

Vera Dawson

Mary Day

Jane Dew

Elizabeth Elvin

Diana Gill

Mavis Graham

Jackey Hill

Lyn Hughes

Heidi Jenkins

Phillippa Kendall

Jane Lemon

Moyra McNeill

Jan Messent

Peggy Northen

Tryphena Orchard

Jennie Parry

Pat Phillpott

Eileen Plumbridge

Kit Pyman

Dorothy Reglar

Ann Sparkes

Edwina Stacey

Celia Stanley

Angela Thompson

Louise Whitehurst

May Williams

CHAPTER 1

Introduction: History of metal-thread work

by Kit Pyman

Introduction:
History of metal-thread work

Throughout history gold has been a symbol of wealth, power, and status, and metal-thread embroidery has always enhanced the rich fabrics that proclaim these desirable attributes. Gold, one of the first metals to be discovered and used by early man, is treasured for its value, beauty and malleability: it was originally associated with myth and magic, and with the worship of the sun. Ownership of golden artifacts bestowed magic powers – in ancient myth the apples of the Hesperides were made of pure gold and, even centuries later, a design of apples in gilded thread was embroidered on the cloak of the King of Mercia to bring him good fortune. Homer relates the story that Helen of Troy's golden spindle could produce only perfect thread, and the myth of the Golden Fleece remained potent for centuries, entwined with the mystique of kingship in the western world.

The first gold threads were exactly that – strands of pure beaten gold – cut in narrow strips from the flattened metal. Gold spangles and hammered gold cut into shapes were also used from a very early date, and examples have been found stitched into the felted fabric preserved in ancient Scythian tombs.

Silver never seems to have had quite the same appeal, perhaps because of its tendency to tarnish; however, once the technique for bonding gold to silver became known, most 'gold' threads were actually gilded silver strips wrapped around a core of silk, parchment, animal gut, or paper.

Wrapped thread required skill in manipulation, and techniques were devised for couching it down and laying the threads at angles to catch the light. With the development of wire drawing, silver wire could be coated with gold to make a very fine round thread. This could then be beaten flat, and later the spiral springs of purls, twisted gold and silver thread, and metallised plaits and braids added to the heavy texture of this type of embroidery.

Like so many other arts, embroidery with metal threads came from the east. The Egyptians, Assyrians and Babylonians have left descriptions of their gilded textiles, and in the Bible the Old Testament describes how 'they did beat the gold into thin plates and cut it into wires to work it in the blue and in the purple and in the scarlet and in the fine linen with cunning work', while the Psalmist sings of a bride wearing 'clothing of wrought gold'. It seems likely that this was woven rather than embroidered, and it is interesting in this context to note the extraordinarily lavish use of metal as a textile; when the tomb of the Empress Honorius, who died in AD 400, was opened in 1544 she was found to be shrouded in layers of cloth-of-gold, which melted down into 36lbs. of pure metal.

Threads and woven textiles travelled to the west in the silk caravans moving across Central Asia, providing the rich clothing worn by the Greeks and Romans. Pliny talks of gold 'spun or woven like wool, without any

wool being mixed with it', and describes a kind of bullion work – an example of which was discovered recently at an archeological site at Kostolats – reminding us that edicts had to be issued against the excessive luxury of Roman dress.

The main distribution centres for textiles, and metal and silk threads, were originally Tyre and what is now Beirut, lying at the western end of the caravan routes. However, once the precious silkworms and the carefully guarded secrets of sericulture were smuggled to the west, the manufacture and weaving of silk ceased to be a Chinese monopoly and was practised by the Byzantines, who made it an Imperial monopoly in their turn and who carefully controlled all related industries; gold-embroiderers were among the craftsmen permanently employed in the Imperial palace.

In pre-industrial days, embroidery was a professional skill as well as an organized domestic activity. Much of the commercial work was done by men, and workshops and guilds existed to satisfy the considerable demand for elaborately decorated hangings, furnishings, trappings, tents, and garments. Characteristic Byzantine designs consisted of elaborate patterning with figures worked in laid gold, shown up against a brilliantly coloured silk background. The tones of the gold were varied by couching it in minutely different directions so as to catch the light, rather in the way the pieces are laid in the famous Ravenna mosaics.

After the conversion of Constantine the Great to Christianity, the manufacture of ecclesiastical textiles and furnishings became an important export industry and remained so for the next thousand years. Embroidered fabrics were used not only for vestments and altars, but also for walls, arcades and doors. In the seventh-century it was said that the whole nave of St Denis in Paris was hung with gold-embroidered fabrics set with pearls. These were almost certainly manufactured in Constantinople.

In time this 'second Rome' declined sufficiently to allow serious competition, and metal threads could be obtained from places like Venice and Cyprus and Palermo, and the use of embroidered textiles spread to all the smaller churches of the west. However the Turkish conquerors of Constantinople in their turn had an equal appreciation of the glories of metal-thread work, and subsequently evolved a form of embroidered

Goldwork box, 'Sea-chest'. *By Diana Gill. The box is covered in turquoise linen embroidered with designs of seashells worked in gold and silver threads and gold kid.*

Gold beaded belt. *By Dorothy Reglar. This belt is entirely covered with a rich assortment of gold beads and sequins, with a decorative edge.*

Goldwork equipment. *A collection of the beads, threads and tools used for the technique of metal-thread work.*

apparel which became the traditional court dress of the Balkans. Echoes of this can be found in the goldwork embroidery on peasant costume to this day.

To date, the earliest surviving example of English metal-thread work is the tenth-century stole and maniple of St Cuthbert from Durham Cathedral. This shows the influence of Byzantine design in the disposition of the figures and in the elaborate lettering, but it is executed in the indigenous manner – that is to say, the figures are embroidered in coloured silks touched with gold, and the background is entirely covered with laid gold. This is couched approximately five threads to

the millimetre with superb mastery of an exacting technique and is one of the few pieces to survive which is worked in the pure metal. The handling of gold thread seems to have been a long tradition in Anglo-Saxon history and, combined with their narrative flair, this resulted in the work which became famous all over Europe in the Middle Ages as 'Opus Anglicanum'. One characteristic of this 'English work' was the use of underside couching, which enabled large areas of fabric to be closely covered with gold thread while remaining pliable. A possible reason for the adoption of this technique was the requirement for a rich background to the

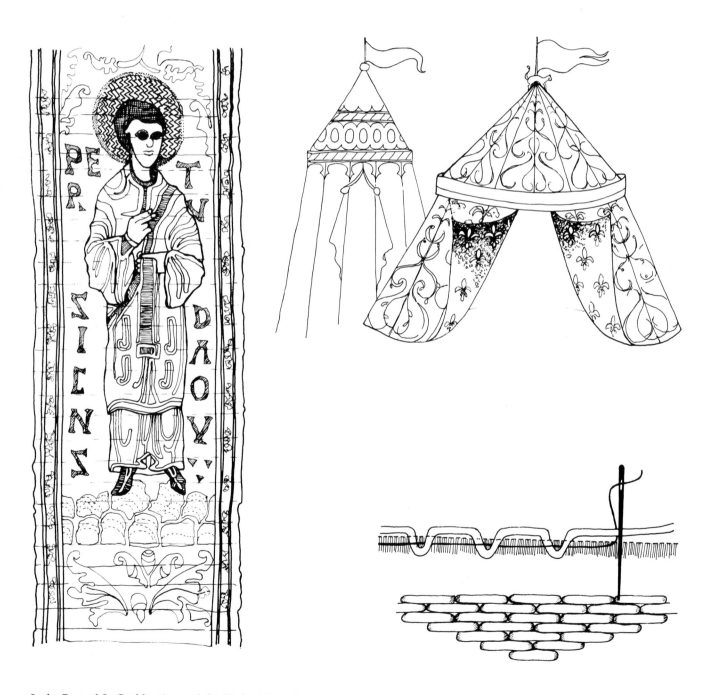

Left. *Part of St Cuthbert's maniple.* Right (above).
Mediaeval tents. Right. *Underside couching.*

figures, in the absence of the magnificent woven silks used in Constantinople.

The splendid fabrics and embroideries of the east were brought home by returning crusaders and must have opened a new world to the workshops of Europe. The rise of heraldic devices necessitated by the increasing use of armour offered a great field for decoration; friend was distinguished from foe on the battlefield and in the jousts by the colour and brilliance of the devices worked in bright silks and gold threads. The widespread use of public display as political and economic strategies promoted the manufacture of costly regalia and portable furnishings of great splendour.

Contemporary descriptions of the Field of Cloth of Gold (1517), so-called because of the lavish use of that textile in costume, tents and hangings, give some idea of the glory of that last meeting of undivided Christendom: intended as a meeting to establish friendship between the two nations, it virtually became an international display of one-upmanship. It was remarked later that many of those attending wore their mills, their forests and their meadows on their shoulders, and for some of them the weight of the metal thread on their clothing must have equalled a weight of debt which took a lifetime to repay. The vestments and hangings were equally magnificent. One cope was described as gold tissue 'pricked' with fine gold and embroidered with pearls and precious stones, and a pavilion was listed in the accounts as being lined with blue velvet which was powdered with 72,544 fleur-de-lys worked in gold thread.

Shakespeare was well aware of the potent appeal of glittering embroidery – Gremio in *The Taming of the Shrew* includes in the catalogue of his wealth 'A Valence of Venice gold, in needlework'. This was probably part of a bed hanging, beds being an important status symbol of the period, and a whole embroidered set would probably last several generations. They are frequently mentioned in inventories of great houses: the Duke of Gloucester owned, among others, 'a large bed of blue baudekyn embroidered with silver owls and gold fleur-de-lys'. ('Baudekyn' was a fabric shot with gold, manufactured in Baghdad.)

The decline of heraldry and the rise of the reformed Church reduced opportunities for the lavish display of gold embroidery, although metal-thread work was used on costume until the eighteenth century. Very little early work has survived, which is hardly surprising when the value of the materials is considered; indeed the wealth of precious metals, pearls and jewels on some pieces must have ensured their subsequent destruction. A large amount of ecclesiastical embroidery was destroyed or cut up for secular use during the Reformation, and at a later date it is recorded that a hanging in Canterbury Cathedral was burnt to reclaim the gold, and a cope was plundered of pearls to pay a Napoleonic war levy. There was a passing craze at the end of the eighteenth century for unravelling and reclaiming the metal from men's embroidered coats to sell for pin money; this was known as 'drizzling', and the fashion lasted long enough for jewellers to make special sets of tools for this destructive pastime which accounted for many a handsome outfit in both England and France.

However metal rarely vanishes, it only metamorphoses; and it is interesting to reflect that nearly all the gold which has ever been mined is still around in some form or another. The goldwork described by Homer on the mantle of Odysseus may have been melted down and hammered into an antique coin, and the scavenged epaulettes of the grandee transmuted into a piece of Victorian jewellery.

Metal-thread embroidery on costume survived almost to the end of the eighteenth century; a royal court was still a glittering affair and brilliant orders and decorations were worn on formal occasions. However, society was changing, and the fashion for English country life and the emergence of the soberly clad business entrepreneur began to replace the silks of the Age of Reason with the broadcloth of the age of industry; a process much hastened by the horrors of the French Revolution which eventually swept the extravagance of gold and silver from the dress of most prudent men.

Since then many other attitudes have changed – such as the value of conspicuous display. Whereas metal-thread work was once an outward expression of temporal power and spiritual glory, now there are other ways of conveying different messages, and the only vestiges left on costume are badges of rank and braiding on dress uniforms. Beautiful vestments and church fur-

Seventeenth-century state bed.

nishings are still being made but the content of precious metal is low, and the effect is produced as much by colour and design as by costly materials.

The light has changed too. The flat lighting prevailing now does not call forth the same golden brilliance that was reflected in the flickering light of candles, bringing life to the scenes so vividly displayed to an illiterate congregation.

Threads also have changed. All that glisters is hardly ever gold, rather it is metallised rayon or some gilded man-made fibre, and there is a variety of sparkling threads available now that the ancient world could never have imagined.

Materials for Goldwork today embrace all kinds of shining embroidery threads, together with knitting and crochet threads with metallised effects and the new glittering threads for machine embroidery. Added to these are cords and braids, gilded leather and a vast range of beads, sequins, jewels and stones.

Opposite. **PULLED THREAD WORK WITH GOLD THREADS: Sample.** *By Eileen Plumbridge. A design based on cordon trees executed in pulled thread work technique using a thin gold passing thread, together with couched Jap gold, and other gold threads.*

Below. **LAIDWORK WITH METAL THREADS: 'The Shape of Israel'.** *By Allison Blair. A panel embroidered in silk on silk fabric, with touches of metal threads.*

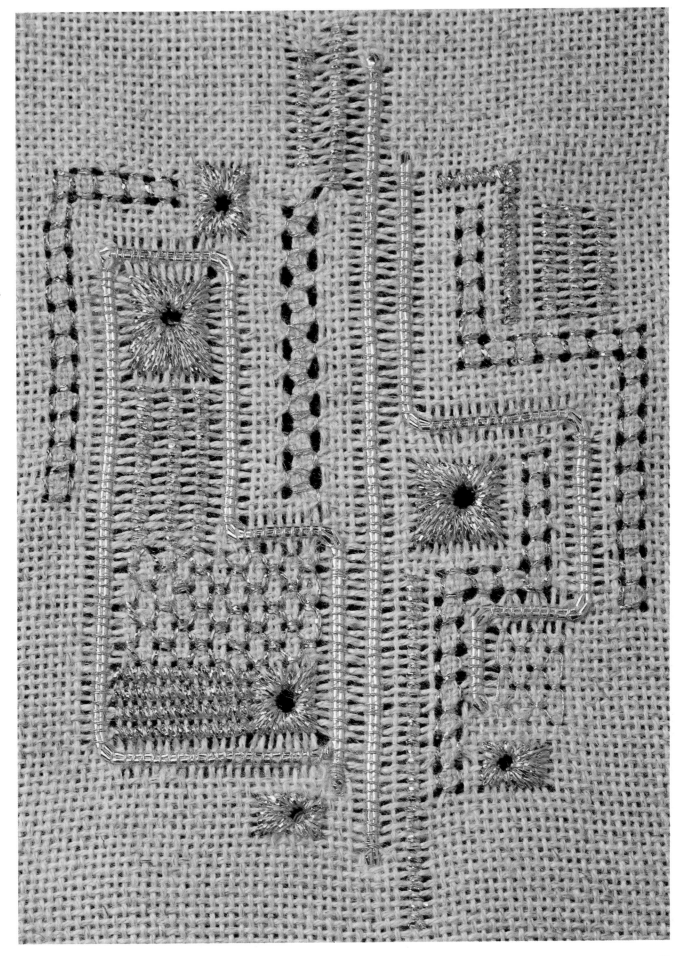

'Gold and Silver Embroidery' describes the present-day development of this fascinating technique. It begins with the basic methods of traditional metal-thread work, and then explores the possibilities of the new materials. The use of modern Goldwork is shown combined with such embroidery techniques as Patchwork, Laidwork, Canvas work and Pulled Fabric work.

Different methods of Appliqué (which is often allied to Goldwork) are explained and illustrated, using both hand and machine embroidery, together with ways of transferring designs and treating the edges of the applied fabric.

Machine embroidery with sparkling threads includes instructions for working free embroidery as well as adapting automatic patterns, couching thick threads, and making circular patterns. This section also includes ideas for belts, cushions, boxes, and various kinds of household linen.

Lettering is another art which has long been allied to Goldwork, and there is a short section on the principles of design, and ideas for combining letters and designing monograms.

Church work has traditionally been executed in the most costly and rare materials, but today the value of the work often lies more in the excellence of the design. A section on designing for the Church provides useful guidelines, and is illustrated by a description of the execution of a commission for an altar frontal from the original conception to the final placement. There is also a pattern chart and making-up instructions for a modern chasuble.

Beading, a subject on its own, also brings a further touch of brilliance to metal-thread work. Different types of beads are discussed, and beading methods are explained and illustrated, with a further description of the art of tambour beading.

Metal-thread work is still a viable technique today, but whereas the true metal still costs a great deal and requires a skillful technique for application, the new man-made gold and silver threads are vastly malleable and versatile and easy to use (some may even be washed and ironed). This book illustrates many ideas for new applications of this ancient and historic craft.

Traditional design in couched silver braid on peasant costume.

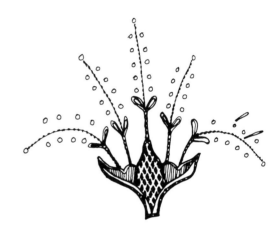

Typical small motif used for powdering. Diaper silk and gold with couched gold and spangles.

CHAPTER 2

Goldwork: Techniques of metal thread embroidery

by Valerie Campbell-Harding

Development and uses of metal-threads – Design – Fabrics –
Sewing threads – Metal threads – Equipment and materials –
Framing-up – Transferring the design to the fabric – Padding –
Couching metal threads – Or nué – Sewing purls

Development and uses of metal threads

Metal 'thread' for embroidery has always been subject to technical improvement, mostly undertaken in order to reduce the cost, and the different types of thread have inevitably brought about changes in their use.

As soon as the technique of bonding gold over silver was discovered, the original pure beaten gold flat strip developed into gilded silver strip. Gilded silver could also be drawn into wire, and this also was beaten flat and spiralled around a core.

Such heavy and costly thread was laid on the surface of a fabric and held down with silk. These couching stitches were exactly spaced and formed regular diaper patterns, adding much interest to the work. In underside couching, a strong linen thread pulled tiny loops of the gold thread through to the back, leaving dimples on the front which divided the golden surface into facets. In the east a loosely wrapped thread called chryssonima was used in such a way that the colour of the core cast a faint haze over the gold.

This early type of metal thread had enhanced the garb of mediaeval people in small ways as well as on the great occasions; stiff bands of embroidery bordered their gowns, shoes were covered with gold mesh, and plaits were encased in long silken tubes ornamented with gold and silver cord.

In the sixteenth century a great technical advance, the invention of the steel draw-plate, made possible the production of fine wires of regular diameter. This led to the development of silver gilt passing threads which could be stitched through a fabric, and which eventually evolved into silver and gold lace. When the fine wires were beaten out, they could be made into the finest and lightest wrapped 'sewing gold' with an orange silk core.

The springy 'purl' which came in many sizes and textures, and consisted of the finest wire twisted to form a tube, could be cut up and applied like a bead, or coiled into circles or loops. Although most purl was the familiar silver-gilt, silk purl was also made which consisted of tarnishable copper wire wrapped with silk and then coiled. This was a cheaper version which was applied to objects where constant handling might spoil the fabric, and where a great deal of purl was required.

As a result of these innovations, couching became more elaborate and rose into three dimensions – threads being couched over string, paper, padding and chamois leather. Purl introduced a new heavy texture. At the other extreme, fine goldwork could be done in 'passing' thread on delicate fabrics, and designs could be worked in metal threads in techniques other than couching. An early European sampler exhibits twenty-six different ways of using metal-thread, which shows the scale of the enthusiasm for these new materials.

Blackwork, a form of exquisitely precise print-like designs in black silk on white fabric, originated by the Moors, became very fashionable in Europe, and was often highlighted with lines of gold or silver thread and a sprinkling of tiny spangles.

Spangles were made from rings of wire beaten flat, and much used for dress – they were made in gold, silver and silver-gilt – even as late as the nineteenth century ladies are reported as 'industriously spangling muslins'. Today our spangles are called 'sequins' and are still used to decorate dress, but their composition now is a far cry from their metal origin.

Gold combined with colourful silk remained a perennial favourite; bright flowers appear with coiling stems of gold in plaited braid stitches; canvas work 'sprigs' in tiny stitches are worked or outlined with gold; single blooms shine from the gauntlets of ceremonial gloves, coiled with metal-thread, trimmed with gold lace and powdered with seed pearls.

Stump work, that interesting three-dimensional technique of the seventeenth century, used buttonhole stitch to form the fine metal-thread into tiny garments and canopies, and the panel itself might be framed with bullion – bullion was a very heavy type of purl, and 'bullion knots' resemble a short length of bullion lying on the surface of the fabric.

In the eighteenth century metal-threads were, unusually, combined with quilting for such items as cushions, bed covers and petticoats. Made of silk or fine linen, they were quilted in a diaper pattern and embroidered with sprays of flowers in coloured silks held in golden bows or baskets: some of the quilting patterns are imitated in couched gold thread.

Fragile semi-transparent aprons were another item very typical of the period. These were embroidered with flowers in silk and metal threads and edged with gold or silver lace.

Men's coats and waistcoats were commonly embroidered in silk and metal-threads and chenille – the ways in which the pockets, buttons and buttonholes are incorporated into the designs are marvels of ingenuity. All-over meandering patterns in couched silver gilt thread were used as backgrounds to designs in coloured silk, but towards the end of the century decoration was increasingly confined to the pockets and the waistcoat.

The light style of the eighteenth century deteriorated in the mid-nineteenth century into heavy metal-thread work upon velvet backgrounds, used on smoking caps, cushions, bags, lamp mats and even tea cosies. However, by the end of the century, the introduction of 'Japanese' gold, which was silvered and gilded paper wrapped around a core, made the thread lighter and cheaper, and embroidered hangings by William Morris and his school show delicate designs merely touched with gold, and the Art needlework of the early twentieth century employed metal-threads merely for outline or emphasis.

A great revival in Church embroidery since the last war, instigated and led by Miss Beryl Dean, has exploited the potential of all the new threads and materials which have been introduced – a study of her work and that of her contemporaries is a revelation in the art of using metal-threads, together with gilded kid, pvc, coloured purls and many other materials undreamed of by the old goldworkers.

Apart from ecclesiastical work, traditional metal-thread work is today practised mostly in the third world on such items as evening bags, wallets and waistcoats, which are sold rather as 'ethnic' products than as everyday wear. However, the following pages show how gold and glitter can be combined with other techniques in most beautiful and interesting ways, and that we have by no means come to the end of a technique which has been a delight to mankind ever since the discovery of precious metals.

DESIGN

Any type of design is suitable for metal-thread embroidery because it is an adaptable technique and suits both geometric or free-flowing designs equally well. Nowadays metal-threads are combined with coloured stitchery, often only occupying a small part of the whole. However one must be careful to give this considered thought and not just throw on a few gold threads, as 'cheap and quick' metal-thread work is unattractive. Aim for simplicity and richness. When designing for clothes and vestments, which should hang softly and drape well, beware of using too much metal-thread work as it can make the fabric heavy and stiff.

FABRICS

Because the threads are fairly heavy, the ground fabric should be strong and closely woven. This is backed, if necessary, with a cotton or linen fabric to support the weight and avoid puckering. Silks look beautiful with metal threads, for their sheen acts as a foil to them, but they are expensive and substitutes may often be found among furnishing fabrics – including man-made fabrics if the quality is good enough – and even scrim and organza can be used so long as the finest threads are used with them.

Try to avoid brocades, damasks and patterned fabrics, which vie for attention with the embroidery.

Fabrics that are unsuitable for work solely with metal-threads can be used as appliqué within the design.

Below. **Samples of metal threads in general use.** *The threads shown are available in different sizes in gold and silver, and some of them also in copper.*

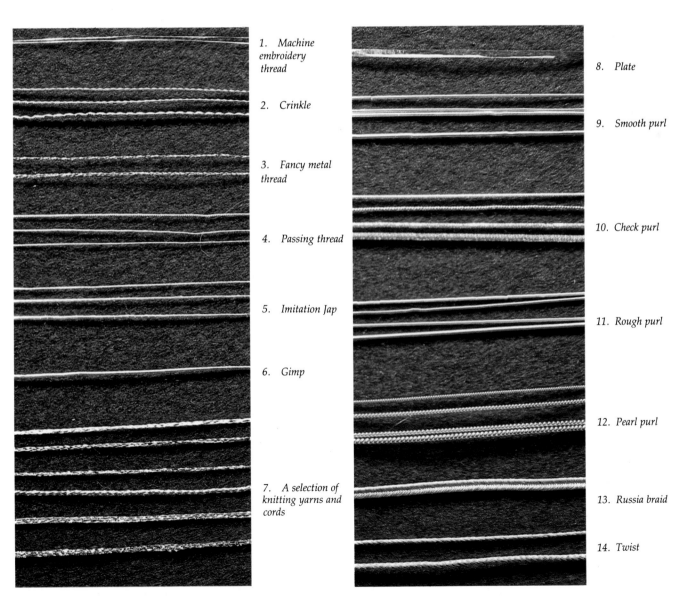

1. Machine embroidery thread
2. Crinkle
3. Fancy metal thread
4. Passing thread
5. Imitation Jap
6. Gimp
7. A selection of knitting yarns and cords
8. Plate
9. Smooth purl
10. Check purl
11. Rough purl
12. Pearl purl
13. Russia braid
14. Twist

SEWING THREADS

Twisted sewing silk or transparent nylon threads, are suitable for couching the metal threads and should be in gold, grey or rust to match them. Fine embroidery threads of any sort can give added colour.

METAL THREADS

Real gold and silver was used for centuries in metal-thread work, but today most of the threads are imitation and synthetic. There is such a wide range that only the most readily available kinds are mentioned here, and a selection is shown on page 17. Some will not pass through the fabric and are used only in couching, while others can be threaded through the needle.

There are many different types such as 'twist', 'crinkle', 'tambour', 'passing' and 'gimp', made in different colours and thicknesses. There are metallic cords, and braids both fine and thick. There is a flat ribbon-like strip called 'plate' which is very stiff and shiny.

There is also a group of coiled wires called 'purls' of various textures, which are cut into short lengths and sewn on like beads, or couched down. There is a thread called 'imitation Jap' which is made by wrapping a very fine gold- or silver-coloured paper around a core of threads, which is inexpensive and often used for couching.

Finally, there are the metallic yarns and mixtures which are sold for knitting and crochet. You will probably wish to build up your stock gradually and there is no need to buy the real gold threads until you are more experienced at this type of embroidery.

EQUIPMENT AND MATERIALS

Frame

Types of frames and methods of stretching fabric over them are described on page 20.

Thimble

A thimble is needed for accurate sewing. Sometimes a second one is worn on the middle finger of the other hand.

Needles

Crewel needles sizes 8 and 10 can be used for most of the sewing. A large chenille needle is required for taking ends through to the back.

Scissors

An old pair of straight nail scissors is needed for cutting the tough wires and threads; a small pair of embroidery scissors for cutting the sewing threads; and a good pair of dressmaking shears for the fabrics.

Tweezers

These are useful for picking up beads and short lengths of wire or purls.

Stiletto

A stiletto, or awl, is used for making holes in the fabric to take the ends of thick cords or threads.

Cutting board

A stiff piece of card, measuring about 6in. (15cm.) square and covered with felt, can be used when cutting purl. It prevents the tiny pieces from jumping about.

Felt

This is required for padding. Yellow for gold and grey for silver.

String

This is also used for padding. It can be dyed by dipping it into yellow drawing ink, so that it will be less noticeable between gaps in the threads.

Leathers

Gold and silver kid are often used in this type of embroidery. As they are dominant, and readily catch the eye, it is best to use them in small quantities.

Beeswax

Beeswax is used to strengthen the sewing thread, and helps to eliminate twisting and friction. It can be bought in special containers through which the thread can be pulled to coat it with wax.

Plastic boxes

Boxes with transparent lids, such as fishermen use to store flies, are ideal for storing metal threads. Alternatively they can be wrapped in tissue paper and kept in cardboard boxes. Do not keep metal-threads in polythene bags as some of them will tarnish.

Equipment for metal-thread work. *A selection of the items mentioned.*

FRAMING-UP

All metal-thread embroidery should be done on a frame. The frame supports the fabric and leaves both hands free for the actual stitchery, and the fabric (or the backing fabric) is kept drum taut. A frame also keeps the fabric at the correct tension, particularly important with this type of embroidery because it is never stretched afterwards, as damp tarnishes the threads. The frame can be a commercial slate frame, an old picture frame, a home-made frame or a ring frame.

Methods of stretching fabric – which is called 'framing up' – on different kinds of frames are described below.

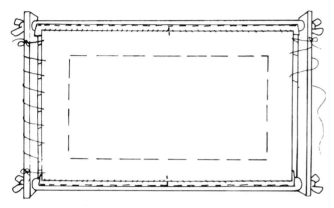

A slate frame, with the fabric in the process of being framed up.

Commercial slate frame

a. Cut the fabric about the size of the frame (which must be larger than the finished design).
b. Mark the centre of the webbing on the rollers.
c. Mark centre top and bottom of fabric.
d. Fold under a small hem at the top of the fabric, match to centre of webbing, pin, then oversew from the centre outwards.
e. Repeat with other end of fabric and other roller.
f. Turn under a hem each side of the fabric over a length of string, and tack. Assemble frame.
g. Using crochet cotton, lace the sides of the fabric over the arms of the frame. Tie the ends at each corner.
h. Tighten the frame until the fabric is evenly tensioned.

A corner of a slate frame showing the backing fabric stitched to the tape on the round bar, and laced to the flat bar.

Home-made frame

A frame can be made of four pieces of wood about 1in. (2.5cm.) square, joined at the corners. Alternatively an old picture frame can be used if it is soft enough to take drawing pins (thumbtacks) or tacks; or an artists' stretcher frame can be made up from lengths bought at an artists' supplier. The fabric is framed up by being pinned, tacked or stapled around the outer edge of the frame as follows:–
a. Mark the centre of each side of the frame.
b. Cut the fabric about 4in. (10cm.) larger all round than the frame.
c. Mark the centre of each side of the fabric.
d. Match the centre fabric sides to the centre frame sides, and fix each centre side with a pin or staple.
e. Pin outwards from each centre towards the corner, tensioning the fabric as you work.
f. Make sure there is no surplus of fabric at the back which might be caught in the stitchery.

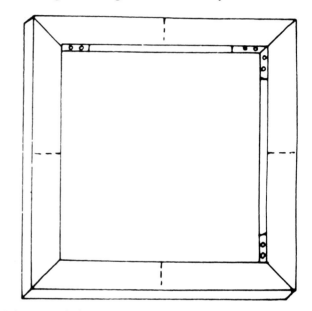

A home-made frame.

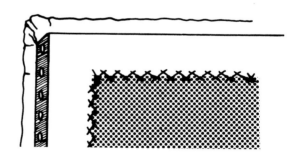

A corner of a home-made frame (or old picture frame) showing the backing fabric stretched on the frame with drawing pins, and the top fabric laid over and sewn in place with herringbone.

Opposite. **Work in progress: 'Calyx'.** *By Tryphena Orchard. The fabric is mounted on a slate frame. The design was tacked on to the fabric through tracing paper and the outline can be seen on the unworked area. Materials used for the embroidery include beads, sequin waste, padded and quilted gold kid, purls and metal threads.*

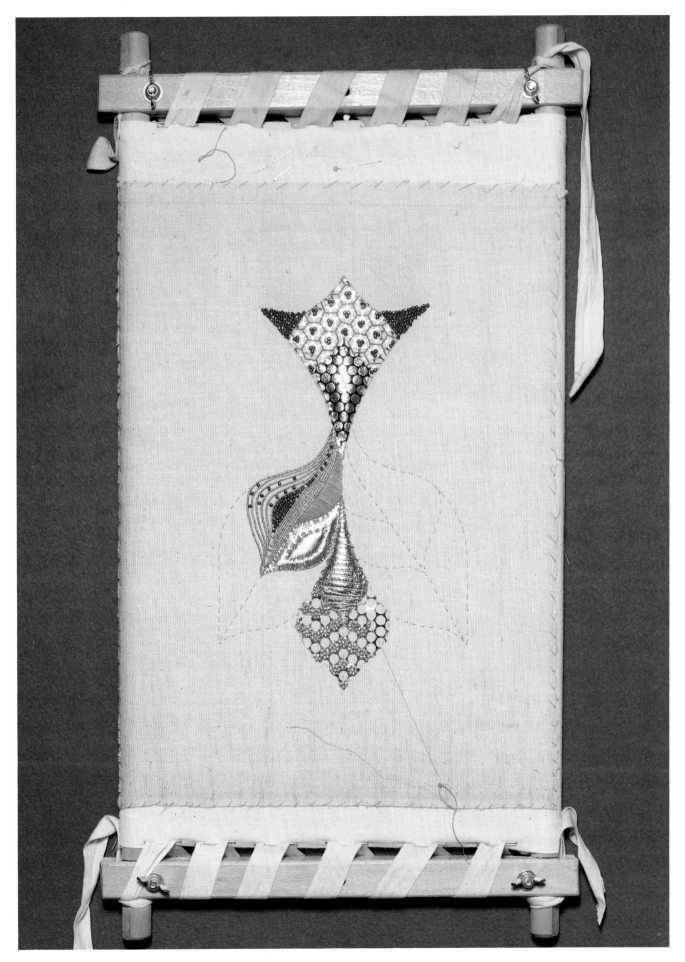

Ring frame

This should only be used for a small design which is totally contained within the ring. Ring frames are not generally recommended for gold work as the fabric will have to be continually adjusted to keep it taut. Always use one with a stand, so that both hands are free.

a. Bind the inner ring with tape to prevent the fabric slipping.

b. Lay the fabric over the inner ring, then press the outer ring into place.

c. Stretch and tension the fabric, then tighten the screw.

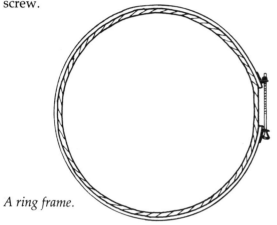

A ring frame.

TRANSFERRING THE DESIGN TO THE FABRIC

Trace and tack method

This is one of the simplest ways of transferring a design. Trace the design on to tracing or greaseproof paper, place it on the fabric in the frame, and then tack through the outlines, using a sewing thread in a contrasting colour. The top stitches should be longer than the underneath ones. When this is done scratch along the lines with a pin to tear the paper which will lift away. An advantage of this method is that, if you change your mind as you work, the lines are not permanent.

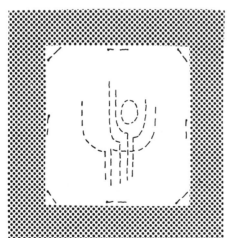

Trace and tack method.

Template method

This is suitable for simple outlines and repeating patterns. Trace off the shape, then paste the tracing on to thin card and cut it out. Lay the resulting template in

position on the framed fabric and mark round it with chalk, washable embroidery pencil or a fine hard pencil. Alternatively the shape can be outlined with fine running stitches.

Transfer paper

This method is not suitable for rough or textured fabrics, and might be difficult to erase if the design ideas were changed during the progress of the work. Use dressmaking carbon paper. Place it shiny side down on the fabric and cover with the traced design. Position and secure with pins or masking tape. Go over the lines of the design with a fine hard pencil. Check that the design is transferred satisfactorily before lifting off the carbon and the tracing.

PADDING

Padding is often used with metal-threads as it increases the play of light on them, and the taut, framed fabric supports the raised areas. It is not a good idea to work too much padding on clothes or vestments, as it tends to look too heavy and solid, and makes odd bumps on the body.

Felt

The area to be padded is marked on a piece of felt and is cut out. Another piece is cut out in a slightly smaller size of the same shape, and then a third piece even smaller. The smallest piece is then sewn or glued in the middle of the area to be padded, then the middle-sized piece over it, and finally the largest. This results in a dome-shaped area of padding which can be covered with threads, wires, fabric or leather.

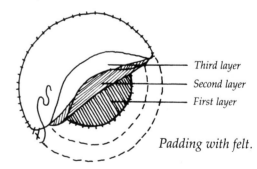

Third layer
Second layer
First layer

Padding with felt.

Applying leather over padding

Gold and silver kid is usually applied over padding. Having sewn down the felt layers, tack the leather in place by taking the stitches right over the shape and not through it, to avoid extra holes. Sew down with small straight stitches round the edge – the stitch comes up through the background fabric and goes down through the leather.

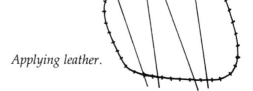

Applying leather.

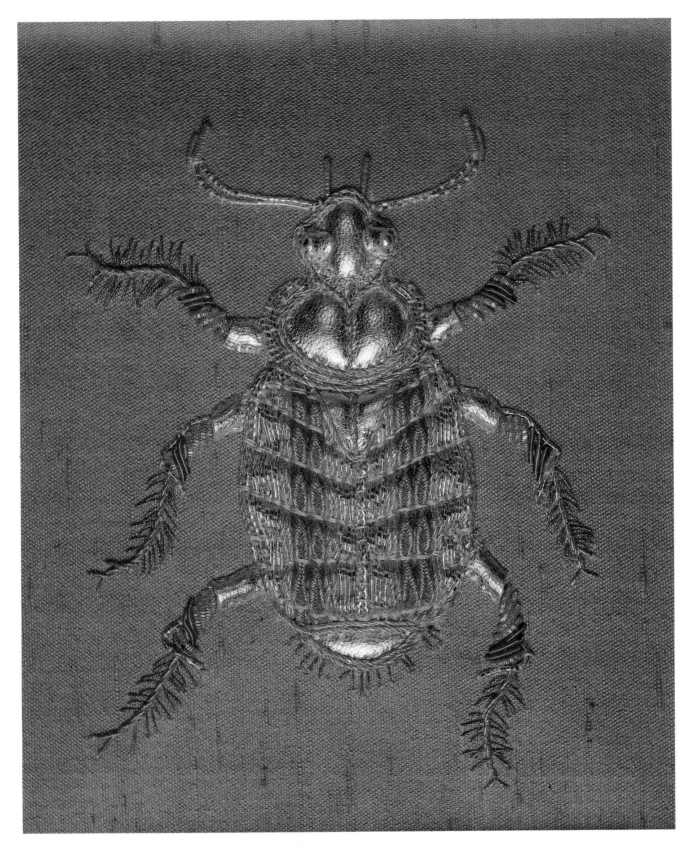

'Beetle' panel. *By Angela Thompson. Embroidered in padded gold kid, couched metal threads and purls, on a green slubbed silk background.*

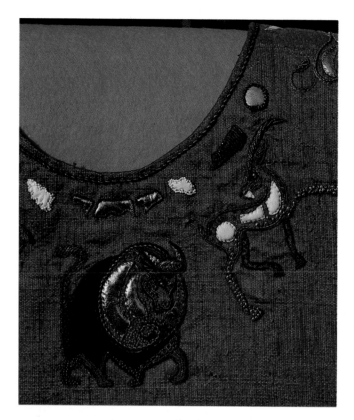

Waistcoat. *By Mollie Collins. A circle of animal designs around the neckline of a Thai silk waistcoat are worked in appliquéd fabric and padded gold kid, with beads and metal-thread embroidery.*

Card

Small pieces of card can be used as padding and give a firmer line than felt. It is a good idea to paint it with coloured ink so that it is unobtrusive, and sew it to the ground with a few stitches. All these forms of padding can be covered with couched threads.

Card used as padding.

Trapunto quilting

Small areas of a design can be stuffed from the back and made to stand out from a design – the illustration opposite shows the background fabric raised with Trapunto quilting as well as other raised shapes formed with applied felt and gold kid.

The fabric should be soft and pliable, and should be mounted on a firm backing which will allow the top

fabric to plump up, otherwise the padded effect may appear underneath instead of on top. Keep the shapes simple and small. Work a close back-stitch around the area to be raised. Make a tiny slit in the back and stuff with lambswool or synthetic wadding (do not use cotton wool as it tends to become lumpy). Push it in with an orange stick or scissor points until the shape is well filled, and then stitch up the slit.

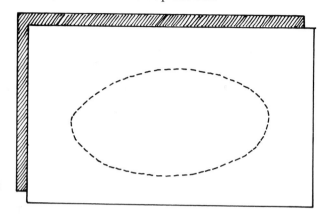

1

2

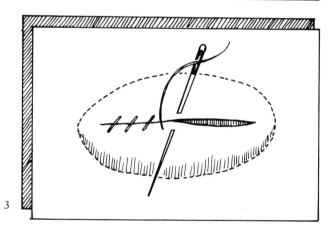

3

Stages of working Trapunto quilting:
1. Stitch round design shape;
2. Stuff from the back;
3. Sew up the slit.

Opposite. **Book cover.** *By Valerie Campbell-Harding. A design based on Honesty seedheads worked on a turquoise silk background. Areas of padded kid and Trapunto quilting are surrounded with couched metal threads.*

COUCHING METAL THREADS

Couching is a method of securing decorative or metal threads to the ground material by means of a different and normally finer 'working thread'. The ends of couched metal-thread are left free and taken to the 'wrong' side of the work after sewing is completed in order to avoid a tangle at the back – so leave 1–2in. (2.5–5cm.) unused at the beginning.

The couching stitches can be worked in a matching or contrasting colour.

Thread a needle with the appropriate colour of sewing thread, run it through the beeswax, and make a knot. Bring it up through the fabric at the beginning of a line and take a small stitch over the metal-thread at right angles to it. Hold the metal-thread firmly (or two together if they are fine) and pull very slightly as you work. Continue with stitches about ¼in. (4mm.) apart, but moving closer together around the curves.

At the end of the line finish off the sewing thread with a back-stitch underneath a future area of embroidery. Cut off the metal-thread, leaving a short length hanging. When the work is finished, thread the end into a chenille needle and take it through to the back of the work. Oversew it in place under an area already embroidered in order to avoid a lump showing on the surface. Sticky tape can be used to hold the ends in place at the back.

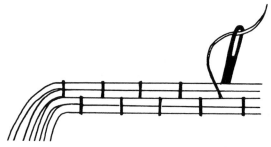

The start. The ends of couched lines of doubled threads are left hanging, to be taken through to the back later.

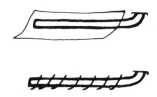

The finish. The ends of metal threads taken through to the back are held in place with overcasting, or sticky tape.

Opposite. **Sample of couched metal threads.** *By Valerie Campbell-Harding. Several kinds of purl and Jap gold couched on to a silk background.*

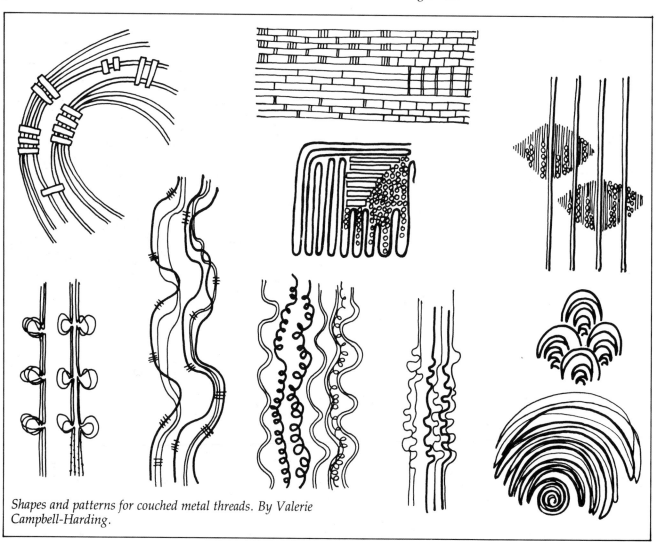

Shapes and patterns for couched metal threads. By Valerie Campbell-Harding.

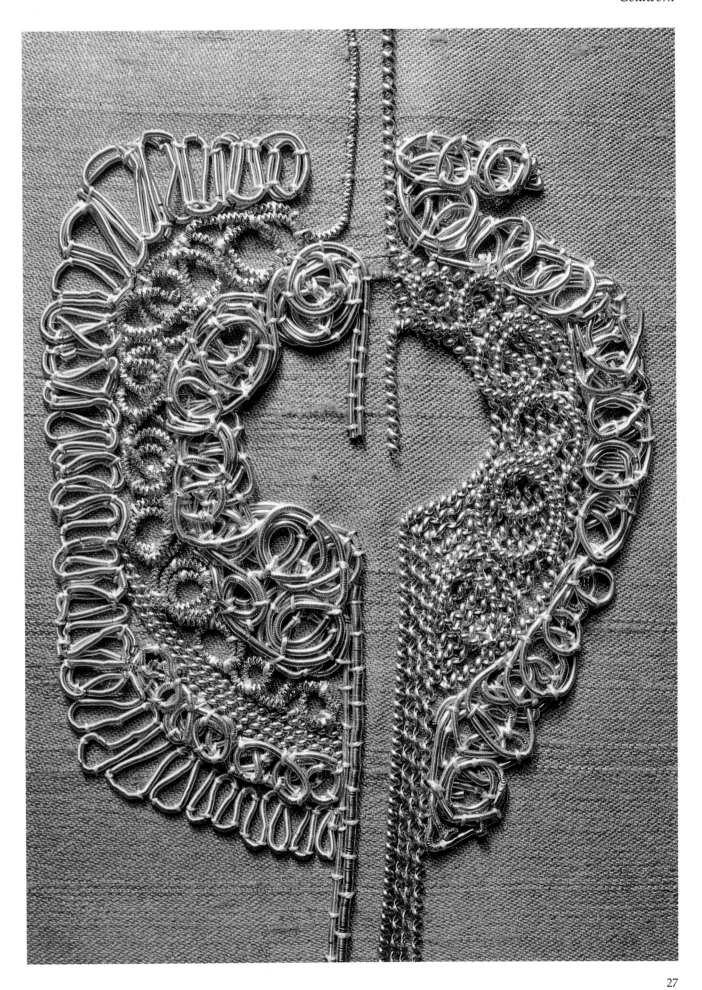

To fill a shape with couching

When you fill in a shape such as a circle, rounded square or a free shape, always start at the outside and work towards the centre to make sure that the shape is accurate. This is impossible to do if you start in the centre. If you are working with two threads together, start them in different places about ½in. (12mm.) apart to avoid a lump. Wavy lines can be couched in different patterns to accentuate the play of light. Where the lines change direction, the threads can be spaced out.

To turn corners

When working sharp corners, you should make an extra stitch at the corner at 45° to hold the metal-thread in place. If you are working with two threads together then the outer thread is secured first, followed by the inner one with a separate stitch. Try to keep the spacing of the other stitching as regular as possible.

To turn threads sharply

When you work a solid area of couching, the threads must be turned back on themselves with no spaces showing. With a single thread this is fairly easy, as a stitch is put at the end of the row, the thread pulled back on itself, and a stitch worked over the double thread to hold them together. When you are working with two threads, the outer thread is secured with a stitch, then the inner one, then both threads are pulled back against themselves and a stitch worked over both threads. Now continue couching as normally.

Another method, when working with pairs of threads, is to cut off one of the threads, turn the other thread, and start a new one alongside it. This method can weaken the fabric, so be careful how many ends go through it too near to each other.

To make sharp angles

When several threads are couched together and have to turn at a sharp angle, there is only one way to keep the point sharp. The outermost thread is cut and taken round the point, but each succeeding thread is cut and taken through to the back, alternately from side to side, so that they dovetail.

A couched circle, showing the double thread starting at different points to make a smooth edge.

Turning a doubled thread.

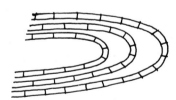

An easy method of changing direction with the threads, which can leave fabric showing through the spaces.

Another method of turning a doubled thread.

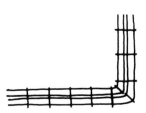

A right-angled corner, with two separate stitches in each thread at the corner to keep the angle sharp.

A sharp point with multiple couched threads.

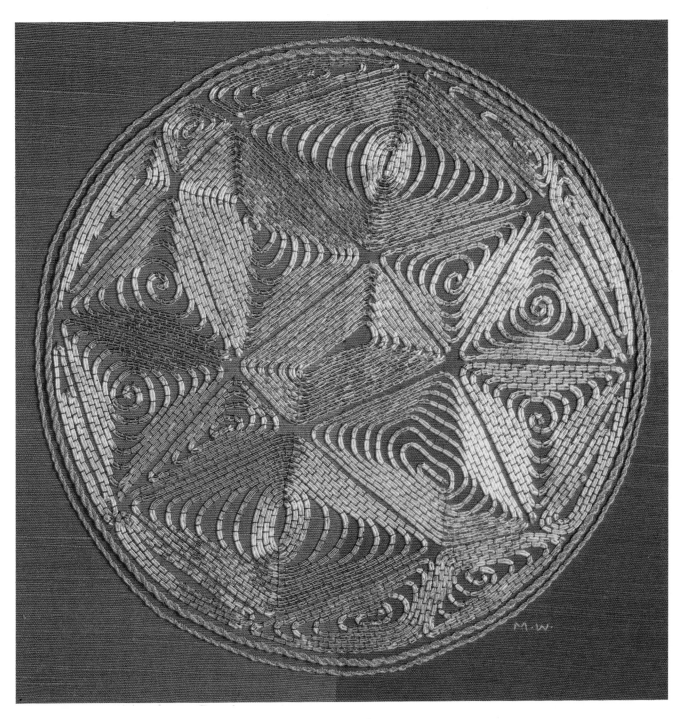

Circular pattern. *By May Williams. A panel on green silk worked in couched Jap gold, the patterns of which throw up changing reflections according to the light.*

To sew plate

Fold back a tiny piece at the beginning of the length to form a hook, and then secure this to the fabric with two stitches. The plate is then folded backwards and forwards, either flat or over string, and each fold is secured with a stitch. At the end another hook is made.

To apply cord

Some flat braids can be sewn down the centre. Twisted cords should be sewn with an angled stitch which slips between the twists and becomes invisible.

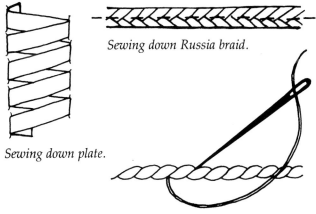

Sewing down Russia braid.

Sewing down plate.

Sewing a twisted cord.

String

This may be sewn in spaced rows for a filling to be covered by couched threads, or in a single line to be covered by plate or purls. Secure the string to the fabric with two stitches near one end, going through the centre of the string. Then sew along the length with alternate stitches each side going through the string, pulling slightly as you work. Bring the sewing thread up through the fabric and down into the string.

String sewn in place.

Couching over string

When you sew metal threads over string, make a double stitch over the metal-thread close to the string.

In basket pattern the gold thread is passed over two strings, and the thread is then couched close to the far side of the second string with a double stitch. Flat areas between the raised areas are sewn with the usual couching patterns.

Basket work is very rich, but it is too stiff to be worn and should be kept for panels, boxes or book covers, purses, and other flat articles.

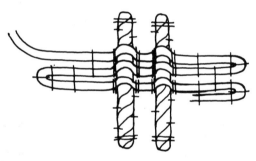

Couching over string.

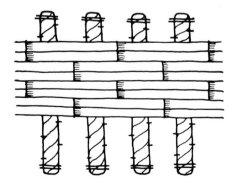

Basket work.

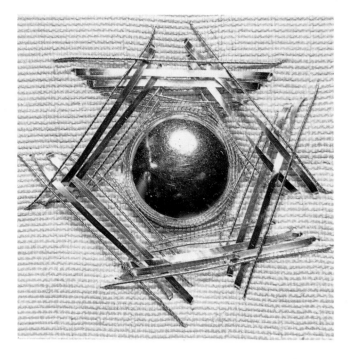

Free use of plate. *By Valerie Campbell-Harding. Plate used to outline a central metal boss.*

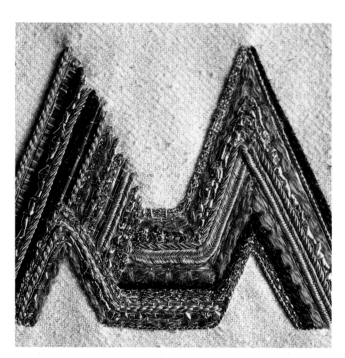

Letter M. *By Valerie Campbell-Harding. Couched cords, plate and silk threads on a cream twill background.*

Couched plate *(part of burse on page 92). By Heidi Jenkins. Plate decoratively couched in a square surrounding a mass of tiny beads.*

Couching over string *(part of burse on page 92). By Heidi Jenkins. A St. Andrew's cross reflects the light from the raised outline.*

OR NUÉ

Or nué is the stitching of metal threads with a fine coloured thread to make shaded or coloured patterns. The gold threads cover the whole surface of the design (or an area within a design) and the spacing of the coloured stitching is varied to show more or less gold. It is extremely rich and beautiful, although rather slow to work.

Historical use

Or nué was worked in England in the Middle Ages and up to the middle of the seventeenth century. The designs were realistic and usually on ecclesiastical vestments. Often the shading was used to show folds of fabric on figures of saints and apostles.

Designing for Or nué

Designs can be realistic or abstract, geometric or based on natural form. They should be fairly simple shapes without too much detail. It is advisable to make a coloured sketch drawing, using gold poster paint with coloured poster paint on top. Trace the design and transfer the lines to a fabric backing, which must be fairly strong to support the heavy gold. It might be helpful to paint the coloured areas on the backing with thinned fabric paints.

Method

Take two smooth gold threads and a needle threaded with gold-coloured sewing thread. Start at the bottom right-hand corner, leaving 3in. (7.5cm.) of the gold threads hanging to be finished off later.

Couch the gold threads along the bottom edge of the design until a coloured area is reached. Leave the sewing thread on the surface of the work ready for the next row. Thread another needle with the desired colour and couch the gold threads with it. The stitches can be ¼in. (6mm.) apart, or as close together as possible, in order completely to cover the gold, according to the design. The stitches should be worked at right angles to the gold threads and in a brick pattern if possible. When the next coloured area is reached, leave the first thread for the next row, thread up the new colour and work the next area with it. Continue like this until the left-hand side of the line is reached, with a new thread for each colour. The gold threads are turned and each coloured thread in succession is picked up to couch them.

Do not use too many colours until some experience has been gained. Work gradually up the design, completely covering the background fabric.

Finish off the gold threads in the usual way after taking them through to the back of the work.

Variations in working Or nué

Although the method just described is the most usual, there are certain variations which will give a more modern look:
1. The lines of gold need not be horizontal, but can follow the contour of a shape.

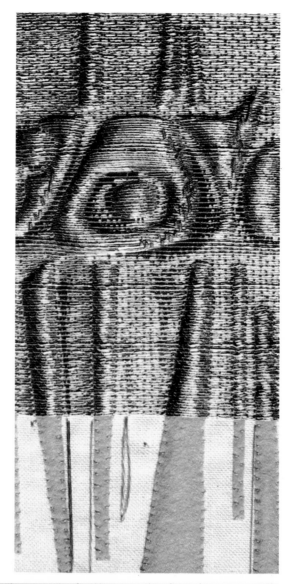

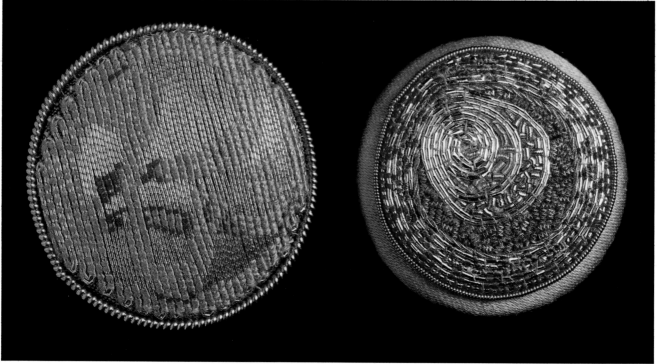

2. Or nué can be used in small areas of a design, combined with other gold work, hand or machine stitchery, or counted thread work.

3. Silver threads, gold and silver threads, or metal and coloured threads together can be used instead of gold alone.

4. The metal threads could be cords or textured threads, combined with smooth ones for contrast.

5. Padding can be used to raise some of the shapes between coloured stitching. The couching is only worked on the flat areas between the padding.

Page 32. **Or nué.** *By Valerie Campbell-Harding. On the left, the working drawing. On the right, the work in progress showing the felt padding in place, and the different coloured threads being used for couching so as to form a coloured pattern on the lines of couched gold thread.*

Right. *Ideas for the use of Or nué. By Valerie Campbell-Harding.*
1. *Lines following a shape and areas of colour.*
2/3. *Gold threads sewn with regular patterns in colour.*
4/5. *Overlapped shapes.*
6. *Traditional couched star, but with colour on one side of each point for 3-D effect.*

Page 32, below. **Goldwork buttons.** *By Jennie Parry.*

Left. *Worked in Or nué, the design was taken from an Art Nouveau brass button. Double gold thread was couched with two strands of silk in two shades, dark for the shadows. Two No. 10 crewel needles were used, one for each block of stitching. The button is edged with purl wire No. 2.*

Right. *Couched gold thread and purls worked on cotton satin, with imitation Jap, coloured silk threads and a variety of check, smooth and rough purl, outlined in very fine purl wire.*

The designs were worked to fit 1½in. (4cm.) commercial button moulds. The fabric and backing were stretched in a frame. When completed and taken off the frame, the work was trimmed as indicated in the instructions. A gathering thread was run around the edge of the circle, the button centred behind the embroidery and the thread drawn up. The fabric was eased round and the ends of the thread fastened off before the back plate was snapped on.

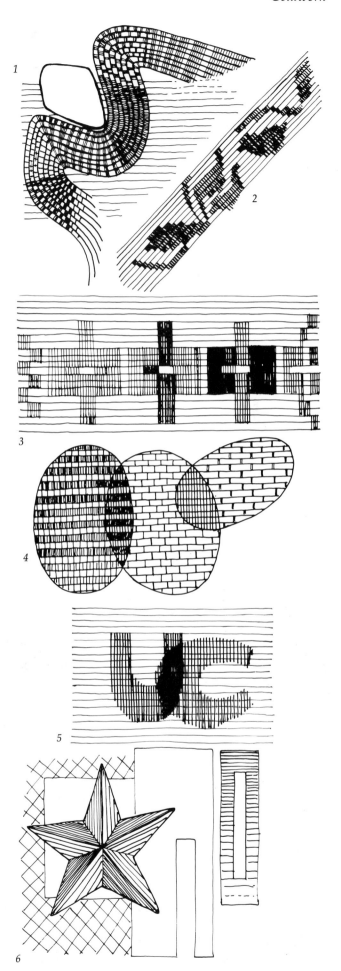

SEWING PURLS

Purls are made of finely drawn wire coiled tightly like a spring. There are so many sizes and textures of purl, and they are so easy to use, that they are an essential part of metal-thread embroidery.

Purls can be cut into short lengths and threaded on a needle to be sewn like a bead. Purls can be used as a powdering over an area, as geometric patterns and fillings, or over padded areas.

Cut the lengths on the cutting board, to keep them together. Use tough nail-scissors held at right angles to the wire. The lengths are not usually longer than ½in. (12mm.).

Pearl purl is much heavier, and this is couched with the sewing thread slipping between the coils so that it does not show. Pearl purl can be used as a continuous length – it is usually stretched slightly to enable the sewing thread to slip into the coil and to remove kinks. For decorative effect it may be stretched even more. It will bend easily, and turn very sharp corners to make accurate lines. The ends are left on the surface, so that none is wasted.

Care should be taken when deciding whether or not to use purls on a garment. Since the ends tend to catch and pull in wear, they are often impractical.

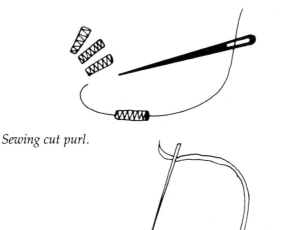

Sewing cut purl.

Covering string with purl.

Page 34. **CANVAS-WORK WITH OR NUÉ: Frame for an ikon photograph.** *By Jean Brown. The object was to achieve a rich but sympathetic frame for the ikon. The postcard-sized photograph was attached to 14-mesh canvas which was then worked in a variety of threads. The main part of the frame is in Or nué technique, with horizontal and vertical rows of gold thread (a double thread of gold for each line of the canvas). The patterns were worked over the gold in a synthetic white and gold knitting yarn and a pale yellow knitting wool. Sequin waste is incorporated into the canvas-work around the inner edge of the frame.*

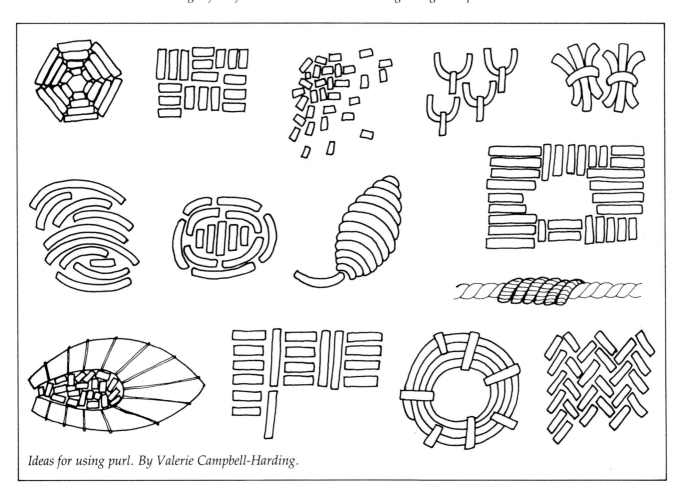

Ideas for using purl. By Valerie Campbell-Harding.

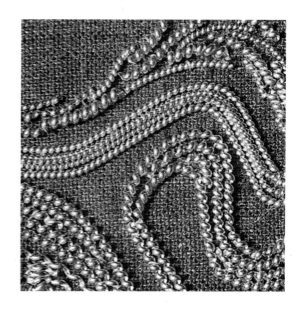

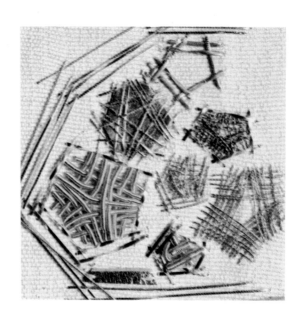

Top left. **Close-up of buckle on page 40.** *By Elizabeth Elvin.*

Top right. **Couched pearl purl.** *By Valerie Campbell-Harding.*

Bottom left. **Couched check purl** *(part of burse on page 92). By Heidi Jenkins. Check purl and New Jap gold couched with green sewing silk.*

Bottom right. **Purl, passing thread and gold kid.** *By Valerie Campbell-Harding. Different materials are used to vary the texture of repeated shapes.*

PURLS AND STRAIGHT STITCH: Drawstring bag. *A traditional rose-spray design was marked in regular parallel lines, which were worked alternately in cut purl and thick silk thread. Different shades of silk were used, with check purl for the flowers, smooth purl for the leaves and pearl purl for the ribbon.*

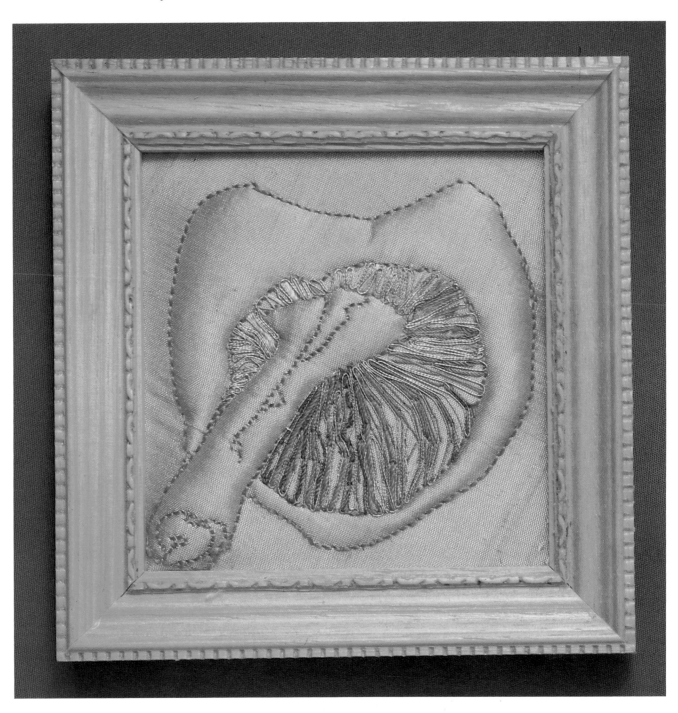

Above and opposite. **SILK AND GOLD LAIDWORK:**
Quilted panels. *By Christine Bolland. Mushroom designs*
worked in silk and gold laidwork and then quilted.

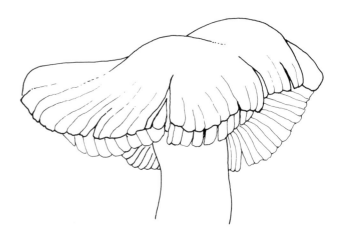

Design ideas for Fungi. By Jan Messent.

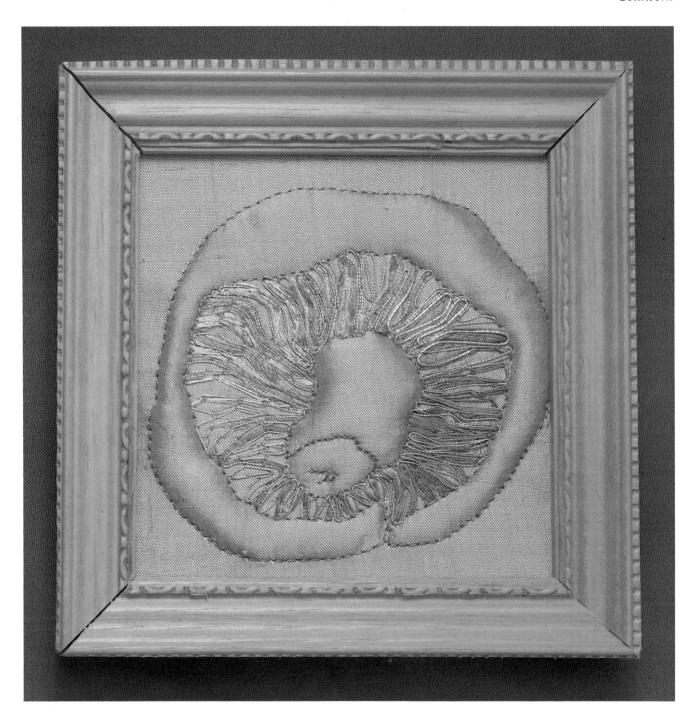

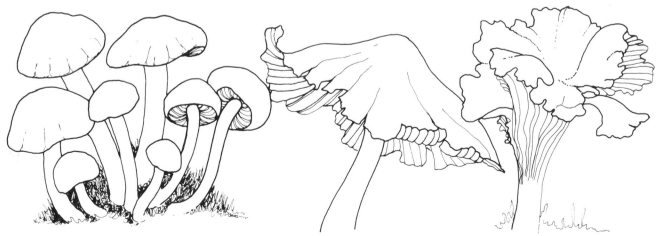

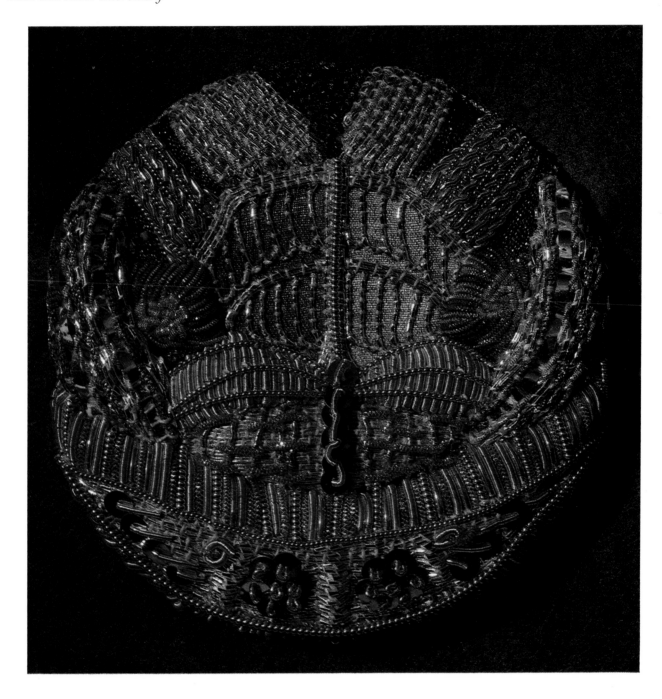

Decorative buckle. *By Elizabeth Elvin. An experimental piece which was worked in a ring frame with a double calico backing. The padding is string, and carpet felt covered with thinner felt. All kinds of metal-thread are used for the embroidery, including some tarnished check purl for the deeper tones.*

CHAPTER 3

Appliqué

by Joan Cleaver and Pat Phillpott

Techniques – Fabrics – Manipulating the fabric – Positioning –
Transferring the design – Hand appliqué – Machine appliqué –
Detached appliqué

Appliqué techniques

by Joan Cleaver

Appliqué is the technique of applying a simple shape cut from one layer of fabric to another, and it is often seen in combination with metal-thread work.

As a method of decoration it has a long history. In mediaeval Europe it was used for banners and horse trappings and large hangings; later it was fashionable to apply needlepoint and metal-thread work motifs to a velvet background.

Appliqué has always been used for ecclesiastical embroidery, and motifs cut from silks and damasks were applied to vestments and altar cloths.

Details of applying gold and silver kid, with padding, will be found on page 22. General instructions for appliqué of all kinds can be found in this section.

FABRICS

The choice of fabrics depends upon their intended use. For example, table linen of any kind will need frequent washing and therefore requires washable fabric and a very firm and practical method of appliqué; whereas fabric for a hanging will rarely be cleaned and here the problem is to select one which will not attract dust.

As a general rule, it is best to apply like to like: silk to silk and cotton to cotton and knitted fabric to knitted fabric. In this fashion the various fabrics will react in the same way.

Nets, laces and any mesh material such as sequin waste are very easy to apply invisibly with a small stab stitch taken over the grid of the mesh.

Transparent materials – such as organzas, nylons, organdie, linen scrims and chiffons – can be overlaid one upon the other to create a depth of tone, and the frayed edges can become part of the design.

Metallised fabrics often require much care in handling for they can be slippery and unstable. Some can be backed with iron-on interlinings, provided the heat of the iron is not too great for the man-made fibres. Iron-on backings can cause wrinkles and so should be used with care. Many of these fabrics need careful treatment of the edges to minimise fraying.

PVC and imitation leathers can provide strong colours as well as gold, silver and bronze. In some cases they have a knitted background which makes them stretchy and suitable for upholstery or padding.

Suede and gilded leathers are particularly easy to cut and handle. When combined with metal-thread work they are often padded (see page 22).

Felts can be hand-made or bought and, like leather and other non-woven fabrics, present no problem of fraying edges.

MANIPULATING THE FABRIC

Surfaces of fabrics can be altered in texture before being applied. They can be scrunched up, pleated, tucked, rolled, twisted or torn. Woven fabrics can be altered by withdrawal of threads, or replacement of drawn threads with metal threads or by a thread of a different colour or texture. Loosely woven fabrics can have holes poked through or the warp and weft can be distorted. Man-made fabrics will react to heat and will harden or melt or change colour when touched with a hot iron. These are just a few suggestions – there are many ways in which to achieve interesting effects.

When applying one flat fabric to another it is important wherever possible to match the grain. Make a paper template of the shape to be applied, place this on the background material and mark the warp and weft lines. Register these lines when cutting out the applied piece.

When a fabric pattern has to be placed in a certain way to enhance the design and the grain cannot be matched, the applied piece can be backed with iron-on interlining.

POSITIONING

It is generally easier to keep the applied pieces flat if the background fabric is mounted in a frame. Tack (baste) them in place from the centre outwards, or across the shape. Never tack around the edge as this causes it to pucker. Smaller shapes can be held in place with pins used at right angles to the edges.

EDGES

A very important aspect of appliqué is the treatment of the edges. Different methods give entirely different results. Edges may be fringed or frayed or left quite free: the demarcation line between the applied piece and the background may be blurred with shaded stitchery: the edge may be invisibly hemmed, or sharply emphasized with a line of couching or machine embroidery. Hand and machine stitching require a different approach.

TRANSFERRING THE DESIGN
Template method

A template is a master shape cut out in card to enable identical shapes to be marked on a fabric.
1. Rule horizontal lines across the paper design to indicate the straight of the material.

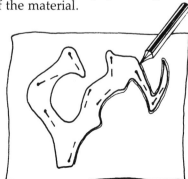

Template method.

'Battle Array'. *By Moyra McNeill. A design based on cars on a motorway. The cars are worked in shaded couching (Or nué) on silver threads, with applied kid and couched cords. The background is partly sprayed and partly hand applied, embroidered with surface stitchery, and extends out on to the frame.*

Trace and Tack method

1. Trace the design on to tissue or thin tracing paper. Place in position on the background material and secure with pins.
2. Go round the lines with a small running stitch in a different coloured thread.
3. Tear away the tissue.
4. Make a second tracing for the applied shapes.

2. Trace the shapes on to card or strong paper, and mark at least one horizontal line on each template shape.
3. Cut out the templates and arrange them on the background, registering the lines with the grain of the fabric. Draw around the shapes with chalk or washable pencil.
4. Use the template to mark the shapes on the material to be applied; cut out and lay on the background, matching the grain lines.

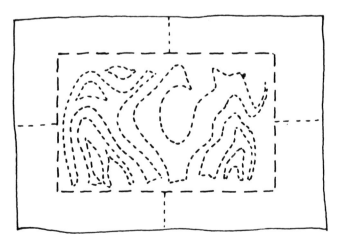

Tacking method.

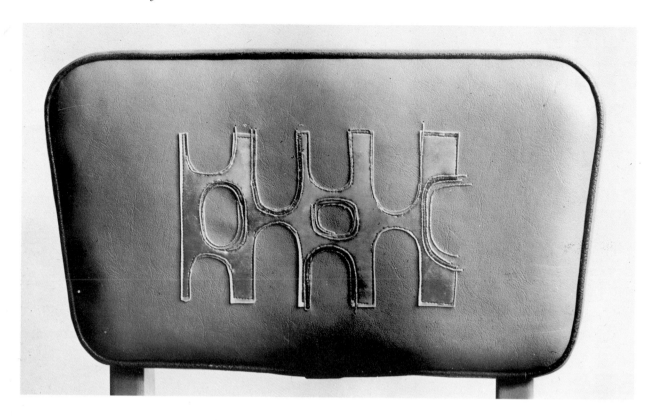

HAND APPLIQUÉ

Materials which fray applied without turnings

1. Cut out the appliqué shape accurately.
2. Position on the background and tack (baste) in place.
3. Overcast the edges using a matching thread.
4. Cover the overcasting with embroidery. Choose a stitch which will adapt to the character of the design – for example, couching will make a sharp edge, and herringbone or cretan stitch will extend the outline.

Materials which do not fray applied without turnings

1. Cut out the shape and tack into place.
2. Stab-stitch round the edge with a matching thread.

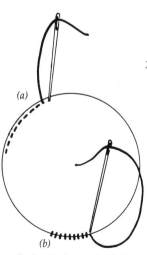

a. Stab stitch, method 1.

b. Stab stitch, method 2.

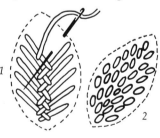

1. Leaf stitch,
2. Individual speckle stitches, which can vary in size and colour. Both examples leave the edges unstitched and are for materials that do not fray.

Chair back. *By Kit Pyman. The basis of this design was a piece of folded and cut paper: cut out in gold PVC, it was applied to fabric-backed furnishing weight PVC with machine stitching. Some lines of gold cord were couched by hand. The upholstery was done professionally.*

Materials applied with turnings

1. Cut out the appliqué shapes allowing ¼in. (6mm.) for turnings, depending upon the type of fabric and size of template.

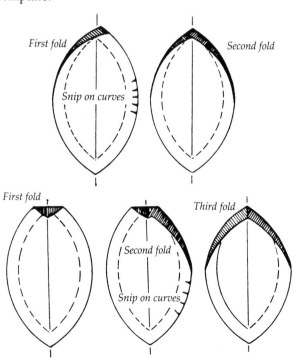

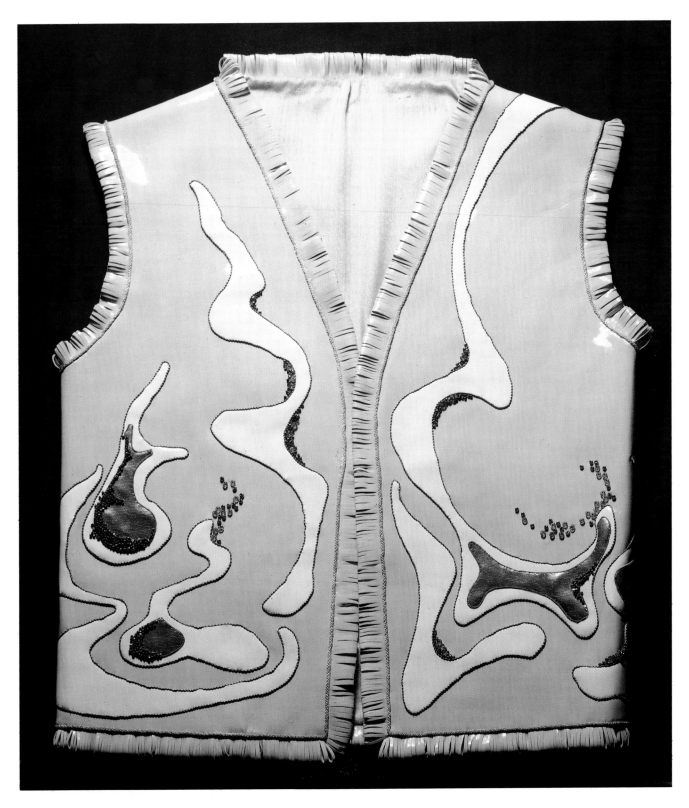

2. Turn under the seam allowance. If this is narrow, it can be folded under as you work. Larger pieces with a wider seam allowance can be stay-stitched just outside the outline; the curves can then be clipped, and the seam allowance ironed or tacked under before the piece is applied.

3. Hem or slip-stitch invisibly in place with a matching thread.

4. Leave unpressed if a slightly raised effect is required, or press flat.

Waistcoat. *By Kit Pyman. Thin PVC shapes in gold and white were applied to fabric-backed PVC and sewn on by hand with invisible nylon thread. The stitching was covered with couched cord. The design was based on an oil-and-water print.*

Machine Appliqué

by Pat Phillpott

Zigzag technique

Cut the shape exactly to the finished size, keeping the warp or weft threads in the same direction as on the background material. Tack (baste) the shape to the background, using the same thread colour as for the machining. Instead of a running stitch, use small stab-tacks that go from the edge of the shape inwards, as these stitches secure the fabric more firmly and the machining covers them. Stitch the zigzag line completely on the shape, and not half on the background material.

Corners

Try not to overlap the zigzag on the corners. The following method will help to avoid this: machine to the corner and stop with the needle on the left and in the fabric. Lift the presser foot and turn the corner. Lower the foot, so that it is now off the shape. Gently lift the presser foot and slide the shape back into place. Lower the presser foot, continue to zigzag, and it will be in the correct position to work to the next corner.

Curved edges

Work a smooth even curve by stopping the machine regularly, with the needle on the outer edge of a curve. Lift the presser foot, move the shape gently into line again and continue sewing. With tight curves you must do this every few stitches. The zigzag will then overlap regularly towards the inner curve.

Below. **Anemones.** *By Jane Clarke. A group of flowerheads in applied nets and rayons. The rayon petals were applied to the background with machine zigzag. The nets are lightly applied by hand. The centres of the flowers are hand embroidered with chenille and beads.*

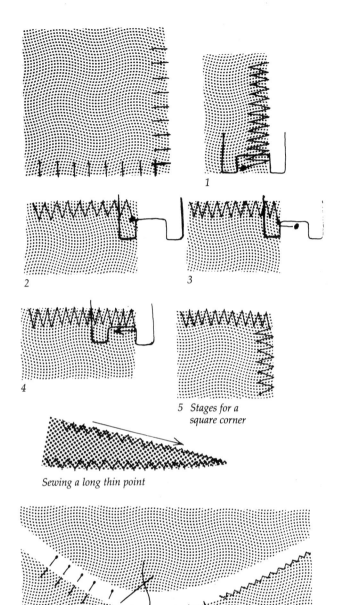

5 Stages for a square corner

Sewing a long thin point

Ribbon stitched to a curve

1. Draw design on appliqué fabric.
2. Position on wadding on background fabric. Work straight stitch around the design.
3. Cut away appliqué fabric and wadding.
4. Work satin stitch over straight stitch outline.

Points

To sew a long thin pointed shape, put the needle position to the right and narrow off the zigzag as you approach the point of the shape where two wide zigzags begin to overlap. Sew back from the tip to the point, overlapping the zigzags right at the narrow end of the point. Gradually increase the width until the full width of stitch is achieved. The straightest edge must stay on the outside of the shape.

EMBROIDERED TOWEL

Machine appliqué is very suitable for household textiles, and a plain bought towel can be attractively decorated without losing softness and washability.

Towelling is not an easy fabric on which to work. Straight stitching is best done with the darning foot in place as it will not push the loops, and it may be neces-

sary to work over each line twice, as often two layers of stitching are needed to make an effect. Try to design the embroidery so that the smoother areas of the towel can be used.

Use cottons for appliqué, and wash them first. Most of the new glittery threads are washable and can be ironed, but check the label before starting.

The design for the appliqué should be drawn out with a washable pen on a small piece of the chosen fabric. Lay this on a similar sized piece of thin wadding and position it on the towel. Work straight stitch round the drawn line. Cut away the raw edges and then, with the ordinary foot in place, work satin stitch around the edge, over the straight stitch, tapering the width towards the points of the leaves.

The rest of the stitching on the towel is done with reverse feed stitches so that they look heavier.

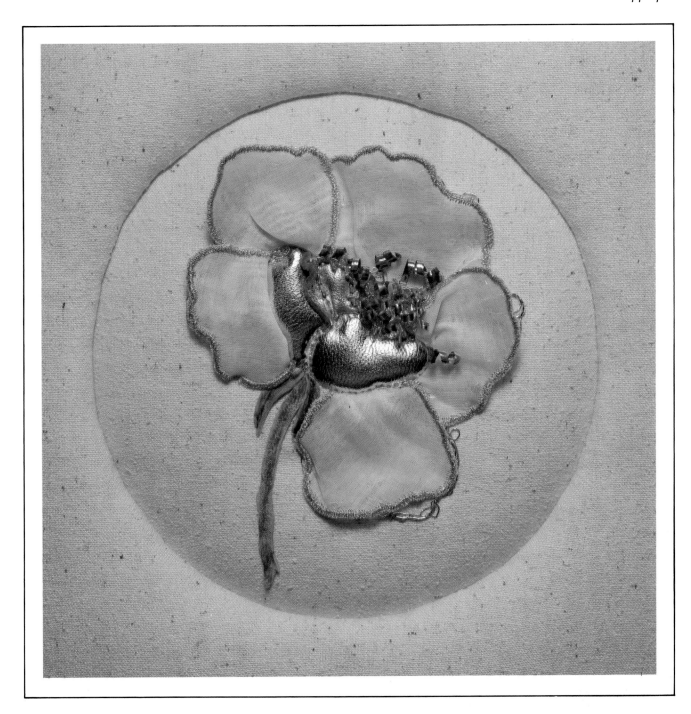

Opposite. **Face cloth with initial 'A'.** *By Angela Thompson. Worked with soft cotton in the needle and bronze metal thread threaded through the hole in the embroidery foot. Straight stitch for the initial, and an automatic pattern for the edges.*

Towel edged with embroidery. *By Angela Thompson. Worked with the heavy cord foot, using soft acrylic cord with metal thread in the needle.*

Towel with applied flower. *By Pat Phillpott. The pieces are applied with two layers of satin stitching, and the towel is edged with automatic patterns.*

Above. **Flower panel.** *By Mary Day. The flower is outlined in metal-thread couched with pink silk. The centre petals are padded silver kid, the detached petals are organdie edged with satin stitch in silver machine thread, applied in place over scraps of pink fabric which show through. The stamens are thin strips of silver plate scraped over a fingernail to make them curl, and combined with random lengths of silver purls to fill the centre.*

Detached appliqué

Fabric to be applied need not necessarily always be sewn all round to the background, but can be partially detached. This involves making the piece separately and then attaching it at appropriate points.

Detached appliqué can be a single layer of fabric, or a double layer, or two different fabrics: it can be lightly padded or interlined, and embroidered before or after being attached to the background.

One of the uses of detached appliqué is to make three-dimensional flower-sprays.

EVENING SWEATER WITH FLOWER-SPRAY

The sweater was knitted in black wool and metallised yarn, and the spray consists of leaves stitched to the knitting and a flower which was worked separately in machine embroidery – it is made of drip-dry, uncrushable fabrics, and is attached with a safety pin so that it can be washed separately.

These flower-sprays can be used in all sorts of ways, on evening bags, or cushions, or incorporated into clothing, or developed into fabric jewellery.

Method of making the flower

Choose a fine polyester fabric for both sides of the flower, and a thin wadding to go in the middle.

Make a template of the flower shape in stiff paper. Lay it on the fabric and draw round it with a washable embroidery pen. Make two tracings on the polyester fabric and one on the wadding. Cut out the drawn shapes roughly, leaving a margin around the traced outlines. Pin them together with the wadding in the middle.

Using the ordinary foot and straight stitch, go round the petals over the drawn outlines. Trim to the stitching lines. Using the ordinary foot and satin stitch, go round the petals over the straight stitch – use width no. 3 – and the fabric should automatically stretch as it feeds round, giving a frilled effect. You can help this by gently pulling the petals in a curve with the left hand. You may need a stronger emphasis on the edge, so work another, slightly wider line of satin stitch.

The lines in the centre of the flower can be worked with a straight stitch or by hand. Beads and ribbons can be added by hand.

Leaves

The leaves are worked in the same way. They are roughly cut out, and the top fabric and wadding are pinned to the knitting, which is backed with tracing or greaseproof paper to give stability. The leaves are then outlined in straight stitch, trimmed, and the straight stitching is covered with satin stitch as for the flowers. The stitchery should be tapered off at the points of the leaves. When the stitchery is complete, tear away the paper from the back.

Trace-off pattern for detached flower.

Evening sweater with flower-spray. *By Pat Phillpott. The leaves are applied to the sweater, and the flower is made with separate detached petals in a fine polyester fabric and centred with small beads and looped ribbons.*

**GOLDWORK WITH APPLIQUÉ AND BEADS: Pole
screen.** *By Diana Gill. This design is based on a scabious
flower, and is worked on deep turquoise shot silk in couched
gold and silver thread of many varieties. Leather and beads add
texture and highlights, and the background is further shaded
by massed bullion knots worked in shades of stranded silk.*

CHAPTER 4

Machine embroidery: with metallic threads

by Pat Phillpott

Choosing and using a machine – Free machine embroidery –
Evening bag – Cushion in machine-stitched patchwork squares –
Belt in zigzag stitching – Circular patterns: table mats – Table
napkins: hems and initials

Machine embroidery: with metallic threads

There is a whole new range of threads for use on the sewing machine which combine the sheen and glitter of metal threads with the ease of handling of a silk sewing thread. They can be washed, ironed or steam pressed and are therefore quite suitable for embroidery on household linen.

This means that sparkling surface stitchery can be achieved with the minimum of time, as any stitch on the machine can be done with these new threads. The most effective ones are satin stitch, zigzag, reverse stretch stitch, and the automatic patterns.

CHOOSING AND USING A MACHINE

No particular machine is recommended, but certain features are desirable:

1. The machine must be electric and have a swing needle.
2. The entire spool case, and not just the spool inside it, should be removable. This is necessary for free embroidery, and for thick threads which will not go through the eye of the needle.
3. The teeth or feed-dog should be capable of being lowered, or covered with a plate.
4. The machine must have a reverse feed. This is easier to operate with a separate button than with a lever or dial.

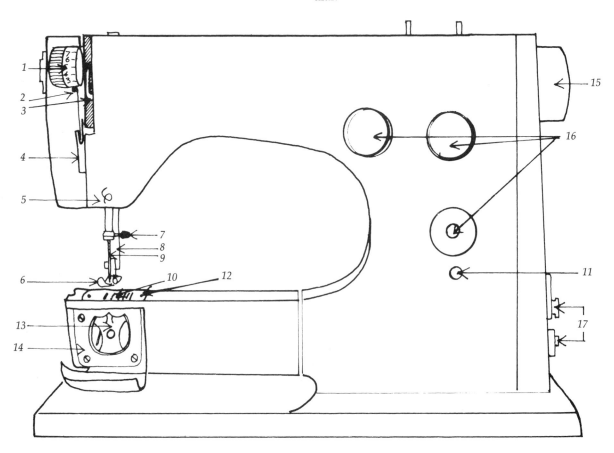

1. *Upper thread tension dial. This is usually situated near the top thread.*
2. *Thread tension discs. These pinch together, holding the thread.*
3. *Thread take-up lever. This moves up and down as you machine.*
4. *Thread guide.*
5. *Front thread guide.*
6. *Presser foot.*
7. *Needle clamp screw. Make sure this is tight, and that the needle is well in.*
8. *Presser bar. This brings the foot up and down.*
9. *Needle. Make sure that the needle is correct, and the groove is the right way round.*

10. *Feed dog. Moves the fabric through.*
11. *Knob. This lowers the feed dog, when using the darning foot or sewing free embroidery (not always located here).*
12. *Needle plate.*
13. *Spool or bobbin case.*
14. *Plate. This holds the spool case in position and is removed when the machine jams up.*
15. *Hand wheel.*
16. *Three dials. These set the stitch length, stitch width and various patterns, and reverse button. They might be arranged differently on other machines.*
17. *Thread guide and bobbin winding spindle. This is sometimes located on top of the machine.*

Needles

A precision needle 705H, which has a curved cut-out at the back of the pointed end, should be used for machine embroidery. It allows for extreme accuracy when the needle goes down into the fabric.

A sharp-point needle is used for most work, a ball-point for sewing knitted fabrics, and a wedge-point for leathers and vinyls.

Needles are made in different sizes and are numbered: the larger the number the larger the needle. Choose one to match the weight of the fabric and thread being used.

Twin needles are available for most machines. They can be threaded with a different colour. Automatic patterns can be machined with a twin needle, but you may need to set the zigzag stitch to half the usual width.

Cushion. *By Phillippa Kendall. This basket of flowers is applied with satin stitch in gold coloured machine embroidery thread. The fabrics are backed with a thin layer of iron-on interfacing because they are placed at odd angles and do not match the grain of the background.*

Tension

The tension of the top thread is usually indicated in small numbers on a dial. The thread must pass through this mechanism. The higher the number, the tighter the tension and the closer the discs grip the thread. The thread only operates when the presser foot is down in the sewing position.

Spool case

These vary slightly – look in the instruction manual to see how to thread it up and insert it. All spool cases have a small flat sprung piece of metal on the side, attached by one or two screws, and there is always a slit into which the spool thread passes, before it slides underneath the spring.

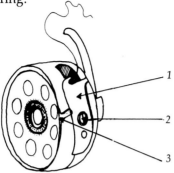

The side of a typical spool case.
1. Flat metal tension spring.
2. Large screw used to alter the tension.
3. Slit through which the thread passes before emerging from under the tension spring.

Spool tension

If there are two small screws to hold the tension spring to the outside of the spool, then alter the larger of these. Turn it clockwise to tighten the thread, and anti-clockwise to loosen it. It is a very sensitive mechanism; make only fine adjustments. Think of the head of the screw as the face of a clock, turn it 'five minutes' at a time, and try the stitch. Repeat until the tension is correct.

Combined tensions

The top and bottom tensions must be equal for normal work. If you use two different colours you can easily see if the threads interlock within the thickness of the fabric. If one thread remains flat on the fabric surface, it is too tight and should be loosened to avoid puckering. Tensions vary on different fabrics, so always try out the stitch on a sample of the same fabric and the same number of layers as you will use.

When zigzag is used, the thread may tighten as it swings from side to side. Loosen the top tension slightly to correct this.

Automatic patterns

The range of patterns depends on the type of machine.

Automatic patterns are particularly useful for items which have to withstand wear, such as clothing, accessories and table linen. Do not put too many different patterns together; try to select those similar in character. Do not space every row evenly but use different widths and threads, leaving some larger spaces between rows.

Machine feet

The type of stitch that can be sewn with any presser foot depends upon the needle hole, and the same is true of needle plates. The types of feet which are most useful for embroidery are as follows:

a clear plastic foot renders the fabric visible when sewing difficult curves or close lines;

an appliqué or zigzag foot is for satin stitch. Look underneath to find one with a wide, cut-out groove that sometimes tapers off at the back, making the bulk slide easily under the foot;

a cording foot has a small arched tunnel-like groove underneath, through which a cord or thick wool thread will pass and stay in place while sewing. Cording feet with two or more grooves are available;

a zip foot is one-sided and useful for machining down beside a thicker piece of fabric.

a darning foot is the one used for free machine embroidery.

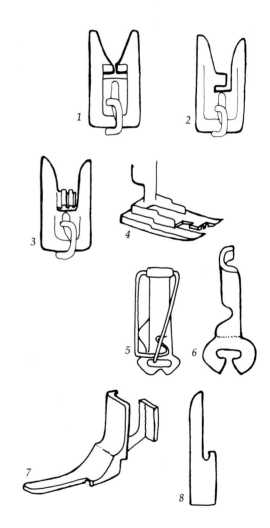

1 and 2 show the underside of basic zigzag feet, where the grooves are cut deeper to take a thickness of stitching.
3 and 4 show a cording foot with two grooves from the side and underneath. The archway grooves are for applying cord or wool thread.
5 and 6 are two kinds of darning foot. There is a spring mechanism either in the machine itself, or outside on the foot as shown.
7 and 8 show a one-sided zipper from the side and from below.

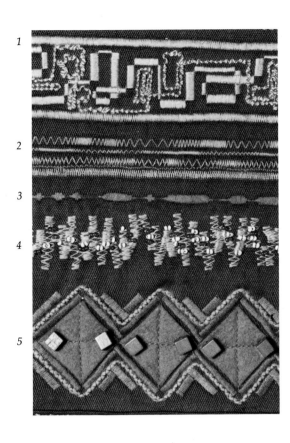

1. *Satin stitch changing width as each corner is turned. There is also a line of straight stitch with perle no. 5 thread through hole A or B in the spool case. (See diagram on page 56).*

2. *Satin stitch, showing the right and wrong side, and the result of altering the stitch length during machining.*

3. *Satin stitch, done with the needle in the centre position and altering the stitch width during machining.*

4. *Zigzag stitch, sewn slightly open and using the reverse feed to overlap the stitches. Beads added later.*

5. *Felt and wool applied with satin stitch in no. 40 machine embroidery thread. The wool is couched on with a small open zigzag.*
(Sample by Pat Phillpott)

Zigzag or Satin stitch

The larger the zigzag number, the wider the stitch. If the stitch length is long, it will be very open. As the length of the stitch is reduced the zigzag closes until it becomes a satin stitch.

Satin stitch can be used as a line by itself, or as a method of applying one piece of fabric to another.

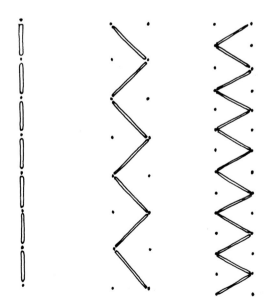

Three rows of stitching show how to bring a zigzag closer together. The row on the left is straight stitch. The centre row has the same length stitch but with a wide zigzag. The row on the right has a shorter stitch length with a wide zigzag.

Fabrics can be applied with an open zigzag if they do not fray easily, or if the edge is to be covered with hand or machine embroidery.

Method

Set the machine to do satin stitch: length short, width wide. This is necessary to give a smooth look to the right side of the stitch. The spool thread must be a little tighter and stay underneath the fabric. Tissue paper, placed underneath, helps to keep fine fabrics flat.

For an angular, geometric design, try altering the width of a stitch when you turn a corner, by leaving the needle in the fabric, lifting the presser foot and changing the width. Turning the needle on the inside rather than the outside of a corner gives a different look.

Altering width

Try altering the width of the stitch while the work is in progress, first in a straight line then in a curve. It will not damage the machine to do this while it is running, it is only when the needle is stationary in the fabric that the width must not be altered. If the needle position is in the middle of the stitch, it will change width equally on each side – if the needle position is on the left or the right, it will remain level on that side.

Altering length

The length of the stitch can be altered while working. This will bring the stitches closer or further apart, but the width will remain the same. Either the width or the length can be altered, but not both at the same time.

Wrong side

The uneven tension on the wrong side of a zigzag line can give very interesting effects, especially if two colours have been used. Try turning the fabric over to bring the wrong side to the top.

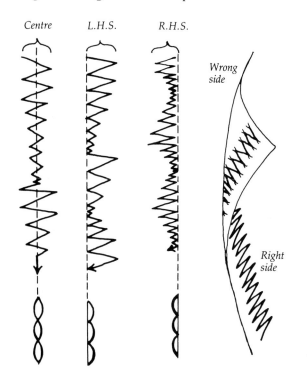

A machine with a needle position control can give a wider variety of zigzag patterns.
The diagram on the right shows a good tension for a perfect satin stitch used as surface decoration. Tension must be slightly looser on top, so that the spool thread stays underneath the fabric.

Using thick thread

Threads too thick to go through the eye of the needle can either be applied to the surface of the fabric with straight stitching or zigzag, like a cord, or can be wound in the spool and worked from the back.

It is worth investing in an extra spool case especially for embroidery. Then the tension can be altered to suit the stitchery, and the regular spool kept for other work.

To stitch thick threads on the right side

Adjust the machine to wide and open zigzag stitch. Use a no. 40 sewing cotton on top and on the spool. Slide the thick thread up through the slit in the presser foot so that it comes through the hole. Lower the presser foot and start stitching, guiding the thick thread along and being careful not to pull on it.

To stitch thick threads from the wrong side

Thick threads can be wound on the spool, and used with a no. 40 sewing cotton threaded in the needle. The fabric is worked from the back and the thick thread stays underneath, on the right side.

Wind the thread on the spool. Then, holding it as shown on page 60, far right, pass the end of the thread

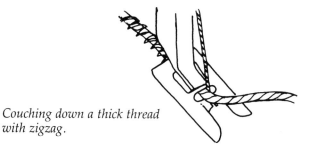

Couching down a thick thread with zigzag.

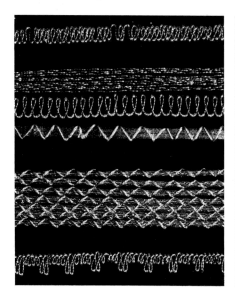

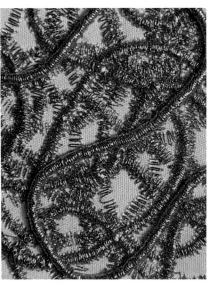

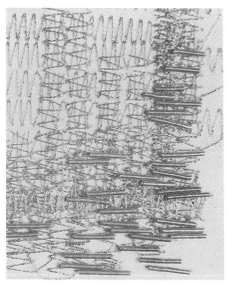

Samples. *By Valerie Campbell-Harding.*
1. Automatic patterns with metal-thread wound on to the bobbin, and zigzag stitching holding down Jap thread and plate.

2. Zigzag stitching using the pressure foot. Bottom layer plain zigzag, middle layer zigzag over cord, top layer wrapped string.

3. Zigzag stitching using the pressure foot, smooth purl added by hand.

up through the large gap after the end of the tension spring. Drop the spool in, check that the thick thread flows easily, and place the spool in the machine.

Use sewing cotton no. 40 on top with normal tension. Try it out first, make a large straight stitch and then use a wide open zigzag. This will make a pattern on the right side like a thick woolly rick-rack braid. Different tensions will produce different results.

The diagrams on page 60 show the two basic shapes of spool case, with three holes for the thread:
Hole A is the large gap for wools and thick threads;
Hole B is at the end of the tension spring, and holds medium thick threads;

Single flower cushion. *By Pat Phillpott. This shows the use through the needle of thicker perle no. 8 in shades of gold, for open zigzag and satin stitch. The tapering up to the point of each petal is done with the needle position on the right. The stamens between the petals are worked by using the reverse feed to go back over the same place and then narrowing off to a straight stitch. The centre has lines of couched wool, and lastly French knots are added by hand.*

Hole C is for normal tension. If the tension spring is removed this hole can be used for thicker threads.

The two larger holes allow the thread to come out loose and make loops on the right side of the fabric.

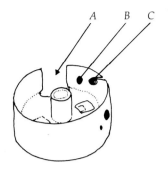

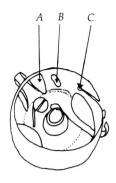

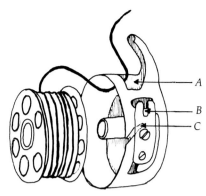

Spool case with tension spring removed.

The two basic shapes of spool case, showing the three holes for the spool thread.

Threading wool on a spool.

Pink silk evening bag. *By Louise Whitehurst. The design is taken from a photograph of sea and rocks. All the stitching is worked from the back with thick crochet and perle cotton threads passing through hole A or B of the spool to give a looser effect. Beads and sequins and hand embroidery have been added.*

Free machine embroidery

The use of the darning foot allows the movement of the fabric in any direction. Stretch the fabric tightly in a small round frame, and place it under the needle so that the fabric is in contact with the plate. Bring up the spool thread in the usual way. Remember to put the presser foot lever down before starting. Secure the two thread ends at the back with light finger pressure, and start sewing with the needle in the fabric, turning the wheel gently before bringing in the motor control. Guide the hoop with both hands and move the fabric smoothly, the speed at which it moves determines the length of the stitch. Pause at points and corners for accuracy. Try moving the fabric sideways as well as in circles and curves. Free embroidery can be successfully combined with formal stitching or automatic patterns.

Evening bag

This bag is made of the same printed fabric as an evening dress, enriched with free machine embroidery worked in coloured and metal-threads, with added hand embroidery and beads. The same work could be carried out on the dress itself as the embroidery is very light – the fabric is a fine polyester silk – and any similar fabric could be treated in the same way. The bag is made more substantial by the addition of wadding and a fabric backing.

The picture below shows a detail of the evening bag on page 63.

Method

Choose a similar weight of fabric with a design of coloured flowers on a dark background. Back the fabric with tracing or greaseproof paper.

Work the flower centres first. Keep the ordinary foot in position, and thread up with sewing thread no. 40 in the spool and metallic thread on the top. Use straight stitch and reverse feed. One centre has zigzag satin lines going towards the middle in gold thread, and the other has added solid shapes like thin petals worked in satin stitch with copper thread.

Next, mark the outlines of the larger shapes, in this case the flowers, with pinpricks through the paper; then turn the fabric over to the 'wrong' side. Wind a thicker thread on the spool, bypassing the tension as described on page 60. With the ordinary foot in place, work round the pinprick marks in straight stitch.

Turn the fabric over again. Remove the paper and replace with wadding; add a firm fabric backing. Work the rest of the embroidery from the right side with the darning foot in position. Vary the metal threads on top, and the colours of the sewing thread no. 40 in the spool. Work from the centre outwards, round and round the smaller shapes. Finally, sew on the beads with nylon thread.

Assembly

Make a back piece to the bag in quilted satin in the dark colour, and use the same satin in bias strips for the binding all round the bag. The flap is stitched to the back piece. A separate lining is laid on each piece before the bag is bound all round. The handle is stitched just inside the opening.

Opposite. **Evening bag.** *By Pat Phillpott. Fine polyester printed silk machine embroidered with coloured and metal threads, with added hand embroidery and beads.*

Two ideas for enriching printed fabric with machine embroidery and detached appliqué.

Cushion in machine-stitched patchwork squares

Method

Choose two contrasting fabrics and, if these are fine, as above, back them with greaseproof or tracing paper when working the stitchery. Use a selection of metallised machine threads in the bobbin, and sewing thread no. 40 in a gold colour in the spool. If a thicker top stitching thread is used then this will have to be wound on the spool and the sewing thread used on the bobbin; and in this case the work will have to be done from the back.

Keep the spool tension slightly tighter than the top tension so that the stitches lie smoothly on the right side.

Work out the number and size of squares required – you could sketch this on graph paper – or if you prefer to be more spontaneous make sure that your piece of striped fabric is going to be big enough to supply a good number of squares from which to choose: the more you do the more economical it is for cutting out.

Cut out the fabric, and back it if required, and work the rows of stitching right across the fabric. Watch the grouping and spacing as you sew, and repeat the same line in more than one place as you build up the design.

Vary the stitches to achieve interesting texture; try straight stitch, simple zigzag and stretch zigzag of different kinds, and for a thicker line use machine couching, covering a laid thread with an open zigzag.

When the stitchery is finished, remove the paper from the back and press the fabric – if the paper proves difficult to remove, run a needle down the stitch lines to separate it.

Assembly

Make a card or paper template the size of your finished square plus a ¼in. (6mm.) seam. Draw in the squares with a water soluble embroidery pencil. Cut them out, and arrange them in a suitable pattern.

Pin the corners together and machine across in rows. Remember to press each seam before machining the next line of squares.

When all the squares are joined, press again. Lay the patchwork on a slightly larger square of wadding, and

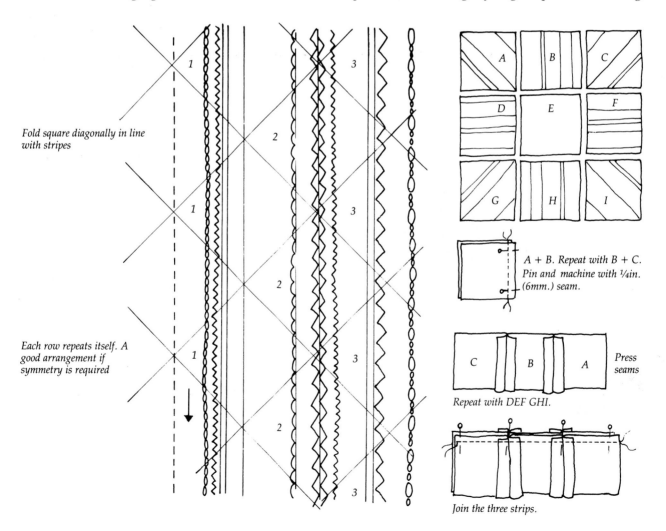

Fold square diagonally in line with stripes

Each row repeats itself. A good arrangement if symmetry is required

A + B. Repeat with B + C. Pin and machine with ¼in. (6mm.) seam.

Press seams

Repeat with DEF GHI.

Join the three strips.

Patchwork cushion. *By Pat Phillpott. The patterned effect on this cushion has been created by lines of machine stitching in metal threads worked on a plain fabric, which was then cut up into squares and re-arranged. Two kinds of fabric have been used, smooth satin and a matt slubbed silk, which give interest but do not detract from the gold stitchery.*

The backing stays flat if worked in a frame.

lay both on to a piece of backing fabric stretched in a frame. Use a standing slate frame, or a home-made frame leaning against a table, so that both your hands are free. Do not tack the fabrics on to the backing.

Work the quilting by hand with doubled no. 40 sewing thread, using a spaced back stitch along the seams. This method gives a softer and more three-dimensional effect than machine quilting. Start in the centre and work outwards, keeping the three fabrics smoothly together, one hand stitching and the other keeping the work in place. When the quilting is done – and before removing the work from the frame – tack around the edge to hold the three fabrics in place.

Surround the cushion centre with strips of fabric using the Log Cabin patchwork method on page 66. Pipe the edges if required. Alternatively you could use four strips of fabric as a frame, mitring the corners (also page 70).

This technique can also be used in stripes, strips or rectangular shapes for other kinds of cushions, or for dress embroidery.

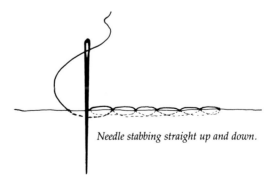

Needle stabbing straight up and down.

Quilting along the seams.

Gold and silver embroidery

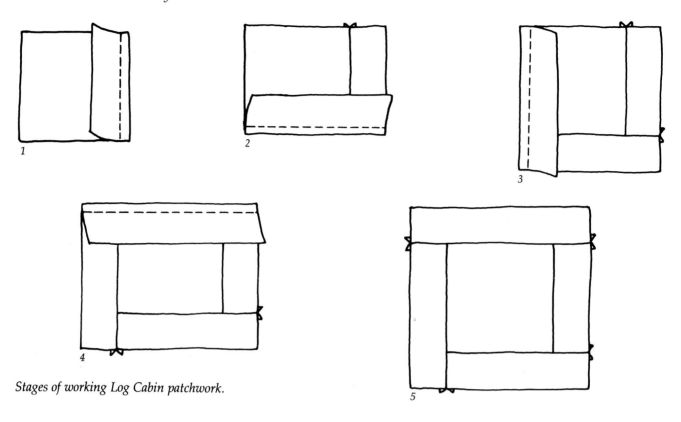

Stages of working Log Cabin patchwork.

Ideas for using designs of machined lines. By Pat Phillpott.

Belt in zigzag stitching

Method

Back the fabric with heavy vilene or similar stiffening, and work the stitchery through it from both sides – thus, when it is finished, no more stiffening is needed. All over background zigzag lines are worked with the ordinary foot in place, a metal thread on top and a choice of colour in machine thread no. 40 in the bobbin underneath. Work from both sides of the fabric. As the tension for a satin stitch is tighter underneath, this gives a two-tone effect on the other side where the loops of the top gold thread pull through and give an edge to the line. Alter the width of the zigzag as you work, and wave the lines. Open the zigzag a little to give a lighter line. Work the thicker lines by couching a thick gold chochet thread down with an open zigzag.

Work the outer line of stitching with the needle position to one side so that the stitching remains straight on the outer edge. Stitch on the beads and sequins afterwards using nylon thread.

Assembly

Trim the belt. Tack it to a lining and trim edges. Cut a bias strip and bind one edge. Cut another bias strip twice as long, bind the other edge, and turn the extra length into rouleaux to be tied at the point.

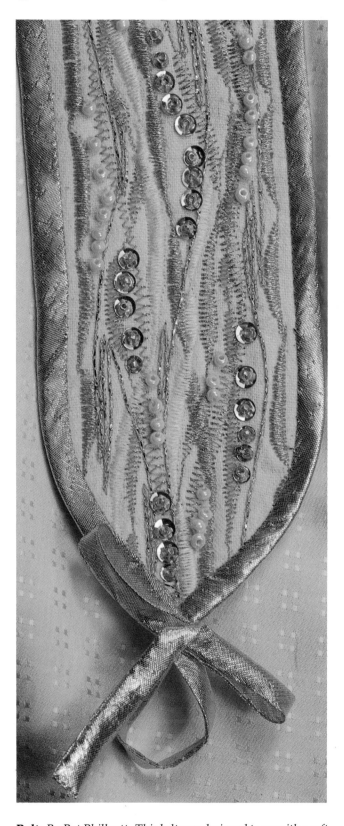

Belt. *By Pat Phillpott. This belt was designed to go with a soft silky dress in the same fabric. Lines of zigzag were worked in metal threads from both sides of the fabric, with added beads for texture.*

Circular patterns: Table mats

There is a technique for sewing circles which is used for these mats. It can be done in semi-circles as well, and can be used on clothes, and for quilted items with wadding underneath. The method only works with stiff or stiffened fabric, so having chosen a suitable one which is strong and washable, either use an interlining or iron-on backing, or back the fabric with paper before starting to sew.

Method

Place a drawing pin (thumb tack) point upwards on the left or right of the presser foot in line with the needle, and secure it with a strip of adhesive or masking tape.

Mark the centre of the fabric to be stitched. Strengthen it with masking tape underneath, and press this centre on to the point of the pin. When you start stitching, the fabric will turn without any assistance. Work slowly with the ordinary foot in place and let the fabric feed around the circle.

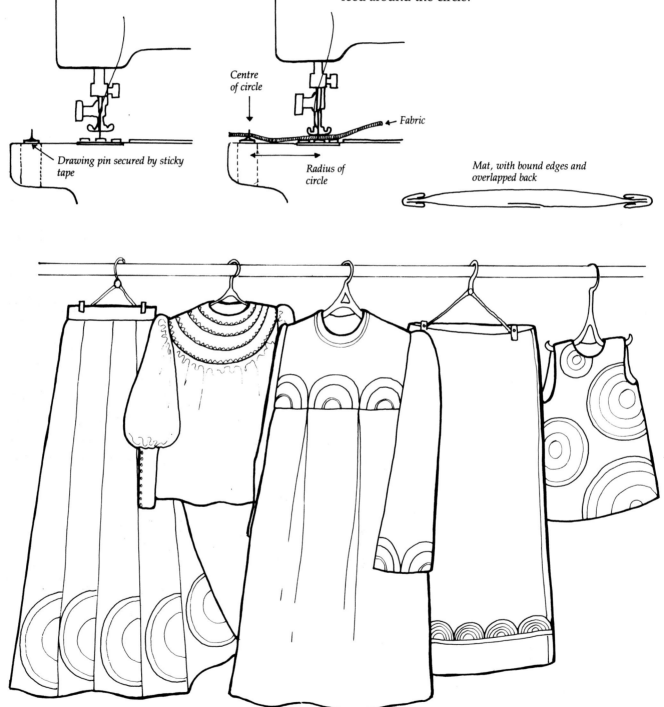

Drawing pin secured by sticky tape

Centre of circle

Fabric

Radius of circle

Mat, with bound edges and overlapped back

Ideas for the use of circular patterns. By Pat Phillpott.

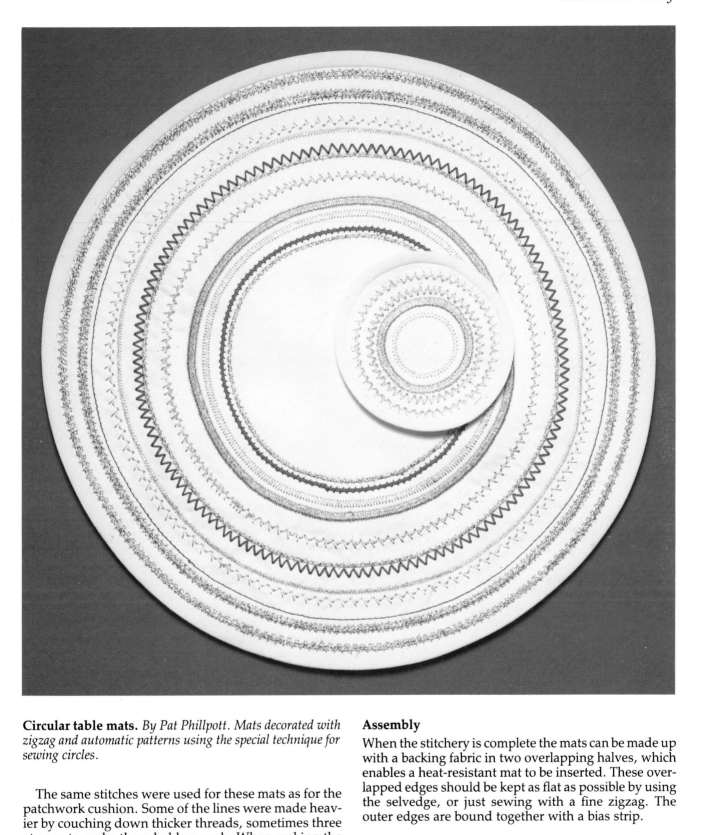

Circular table mats. *By Pat Phillpott. Mats decorated with zigzag and automatic patterns using the special technique for sewing circles.*

The same stitches were used for these mats as for the patchwork cushion. Some of the lines were made heavier by couching down thicker threads, sometimes three at once to make them bold enough. When making the large mat, stitch the first two rows by this method and then use the width of the foot to guide and space each subsequent line.

Assembly

When the stitchery is complete the mats can be made up with a backing fabric in two overlapping halves, which enables a heat-resistant mat to be inserted. These overlapped edges should be kept as flat as possible by using the selvedge, or just sewing with a fine zigzag. The outer edges are bound together with a bias strip.

Table napkins: Hems and initials

As table napkins are generally seen from both sides, it is necessary to have the metallic thread both in the spool and on top. Working a corner, or near to an edge, you will have to use the ordinary foot for better control.

Hems

Allow about ½in. (12mm.) seam allowance all round, and cut out the fabric exactly on the straight grain – draw a thread in each direction as a guide. Turn the hem to the right side as shown in diagram (a), making a mitred corner, and pressing the folds. Cover the raw edge with a thick thread and couch it down with an open zigzag. If a zigzag is used on its own, then the raw edges will have to be turned under as in diagram (b).

Initials

If the initial is to be in the corner of the napkin, use the ordinary foot. If it is near the centre then the darning foot can be used, and the fabric can be mounted in a ring frame. Although satin stitch is used in both cases, the effect is different because of the way the fabric is moved.

With the ordinary foot in place, the fabric has to be moved around as you work – when negotiating a curve, keep stopping with the needle in the fabric on the outer line, lift the presser foot, move the fabric, and then lower the presser foot again and work another section. The stitches will overlap towards the inside.

With the darning foot in place, try to keep the satin stitch horizontal as you move the frame.

Initials often need to be worked over twice to cover the fabric because, if the stitch is close enough to cover the first time, it may pile up and will not then feed through. Use greaseproof or heavy tracing paper underneath, and work with a slightly open satin stitch.

Page 71.
Top left. **Table napkin.** *By Angela Thompson. Worked in metal threads in zigzag, satin stitch and automatic patterns. The hem is worked in zigzag over white acrylic cord using the heavy cord foot with gold thread in the needle. The automatic patterns are worked over six strands of perle cotton using the multicord foot.*

Top right. **Table napkin.** *By Pat Phillpott. Worked in zigzag and satin stitch in metal threads. The initial is satin stitch in a fine metallic cord, and the hem is worked in an open zigzag over thick cord.*

Centre. **Table napkin.** *By Angela Thompson. The tree motif is worked in gold and silver threads. The gold border is sewn from the wrong side, the gold metallic cords sewn with silver thread in the needle using the multicord foot and automatic pattern. The eyelets are worked on an eyelet stitch in fine silver thread.*

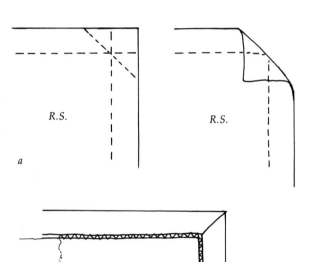

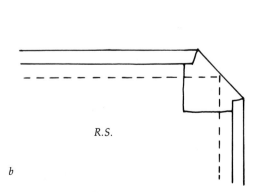

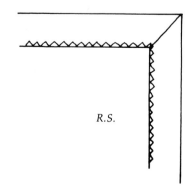

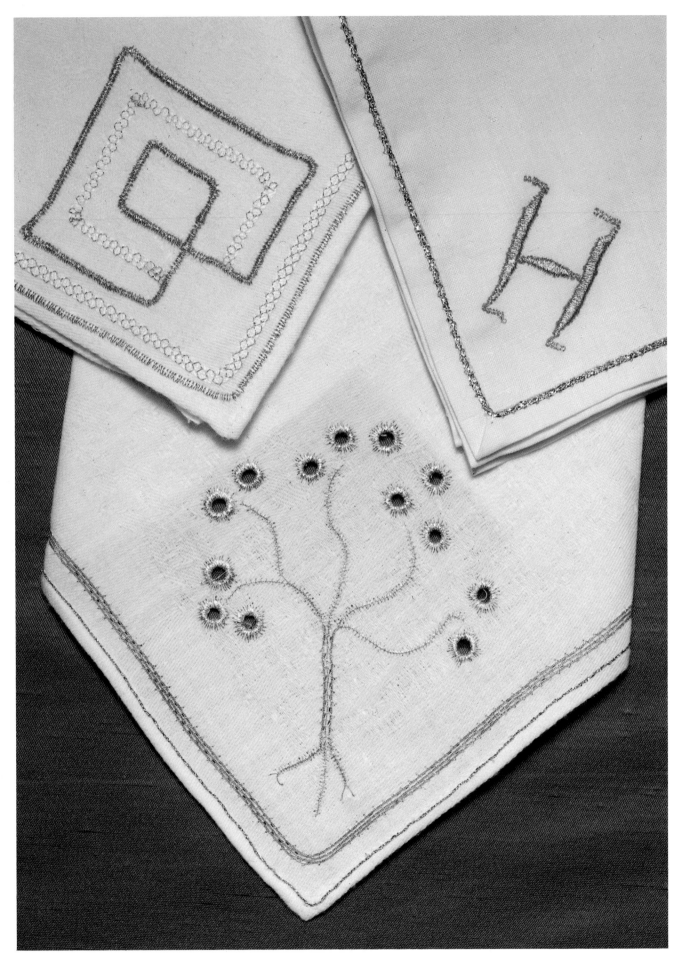

Opposite. **Handkerchiefs.** *By Angela Thompson.*

Top. *Silver zigzag forms the border, and the central motif is worked with a spiral stitcher with a gold thread in the needle.*
Centre. *Automatic pattern border. The initial is worked with twin needles and the darning foot.*
Bottom. *Twin needle automatic pattern worked on the border, with one thin gold thread and one shaded metallic thread.*

Circular box. *By Pat Phillpott. The top of this box is worked in the same way as the mats, using the circular sewing technique on red silk polyester with an assortment of metallised threads. The edge is neatened with a bias strip. The 'flower' is a rouleau of fabric and gold ribbon. The knob is a button stitched through the card, sunk into a curtain ring covered with blanket-stitched silk.*

Ideas for machine-embroidered table linen. By Jan Messent.

CHAPTER 5

Lettering

by Pat Phillpott

Design with letters – Lettering with motifs – Mirror-image designs

Lettering

Letters are shapes. In design they have two functions: the first is to communicate something through reading (they have a meaning); the second is to create visual pleasure by their arrangement and position in a composition.

These functions can be used to a greater or lesser degree depending on the purpose of the design. If the work must be read, then care must be taken not to destroy the words when developing a design.

DESIGN WITH LETTERS

Ideas for letter shapes can be taken from books on lettering, lettering catalogues for printers, titles on bookbindings and headings in magazines. Some letters are graceful and curvaceous and others are rigid and upright. Some are so unusual that they are nearly illegible. All lettering has character, and you must decide if it suits your purpose and meaning.

From the point of view of design, there are letter shapes and space shapes – the space between and around the letters – and both are equally important.

To start with, take simple letter shapes and treat them straightforwardly. Work on tracing paper and move it over letters already drawn or cut out; single-line letters will produce a different effect from solid letters; letters with both thick and thin lines are different again. Pencil in faint guide lines; arrange a single letter along parallel lines, then try the same idea on a cross-grid and lay them diagonally.

Related lines can be added to a basic design – these are lines that follow but not exactly, repeat but not quite. If the item to be made has an outline, then the lines may need to relate to that edge.

For some techniques such as quilting or machine stitching the designs can be left as linear, or they can become shapes for such techniques as patchwork, appliqué, beadwork or goldwork. The design and technique will vary according to the purpose of the item, and whether it is a border or a central motif.

Spacing is important if the group of letters is to be read as a word. If any of the letters are too far apart then the word becomes illegible. There are general rules for the spacing of letters which have evolved from hand-written script lettering. The basic idea is to make each space look equal, although it may not actually be so. Some letters curve widely outwards, such as O G C, and these are placed differently from the straight and upright ones like H I P N M. Two uprights together need more space because they are parallel – N I – whereas N O can be closer because the space widens towards the top and bottom of the letters and appears to fill a greater area. Two curvy letters like S O have to be judged on visual appearance as the space is a very odd shape. The idea can best be grasped if you use and cut out paper letters and arrange them on a coloured background, so that the spaces between are visible.

Below. *An idea for a patchwork or appliqué cushion incorporating the name LESLIE. A series of stripes, drawn above and below the letters, continues one or both sides of the letters up into the first stripe.*

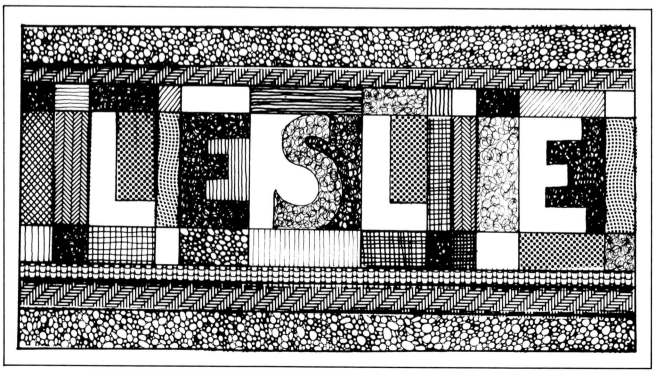

Design with letters forming the name LESLIE

When the name is printed out between parallel lines, look at the size and shape of the spaces between:
1. This space can be very small as the area opens up.
2. This is the greatest space.
3. Space can be minimal as area opens up each side.
4. More space than 3. to allow for straight side of L.

If the letters are not in line with each other then everything changes. Lines can be drawn to continue one side of a letter, and related lines can break the larger areas down.

One difficulty with this group of letters is to integrate the S, as the only curved shape in the group. If all the letters are redrawn as curved characters then the whole design is easier.

Letters re-drawn as curved characters. Dotted line omitted after drawing other lines.

Straightforward letters with related lines.

Lettering with motifs

When the letters are to be combined with motifs like fish, flowers or butterflies, try to make the design look cohesive, and not as though the motifs have simply been added in the spaces left by the letters.

The designs opposite are for a box top as a gift, and incorporate the initials E M O. The letters are not dominant in size, but they could be made dominant in colour or in tone. Gold threads, machine embroidery, applied leather, beads and seeding would look good on a small scale.

If lines go off the edge of a design then the eye is led into the design along them, which is good. If they do not go off the edge, be careful of placing the dominant features – if there is equal space round the outside, the dark and light tones should be carefully distributed within the design.

Letter 'S' panel. *By May Williams. The letter shape is filled with sweeping lines of couched Jap gold expanding at each end round a circle packed with tightly embroidered tiny flowers. The inner spaces are filled with padded gold kid. A tiny repetition of the design is used as a full stop.*

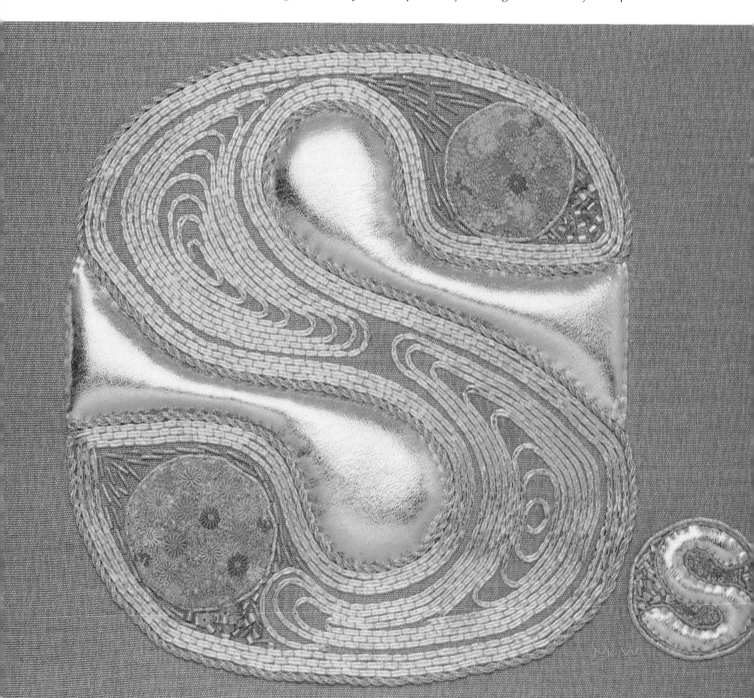

Monograms of letters EMO by Pat Phillpott. In the left-hand example, the lines go off the edge of the design; on the right, the design is contained within the shape.

Ideas for combining letters with motifs. By Jan Messent.

Mirror-image designs

Here the letters H and T have been used as the basis for symmetrical designs. These letters are not readable, but can be used to form attractive and unusual repeating shapes.

Opposite. **Monogram A.S.** *By Ann Sparkes. The initials are quilted on to a cream silky polyester, outlined in gold machine embroidery and couching, and filled with French knots in stranded cotton in shades of peach and rust.*

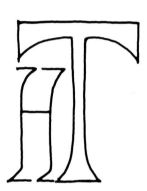

The two letters H and T, in different kinds of lettering.

Two traced over each other at right angles.

Traced, and then folded to trace mirror image.

Final design leaving out small overlapping shapes.

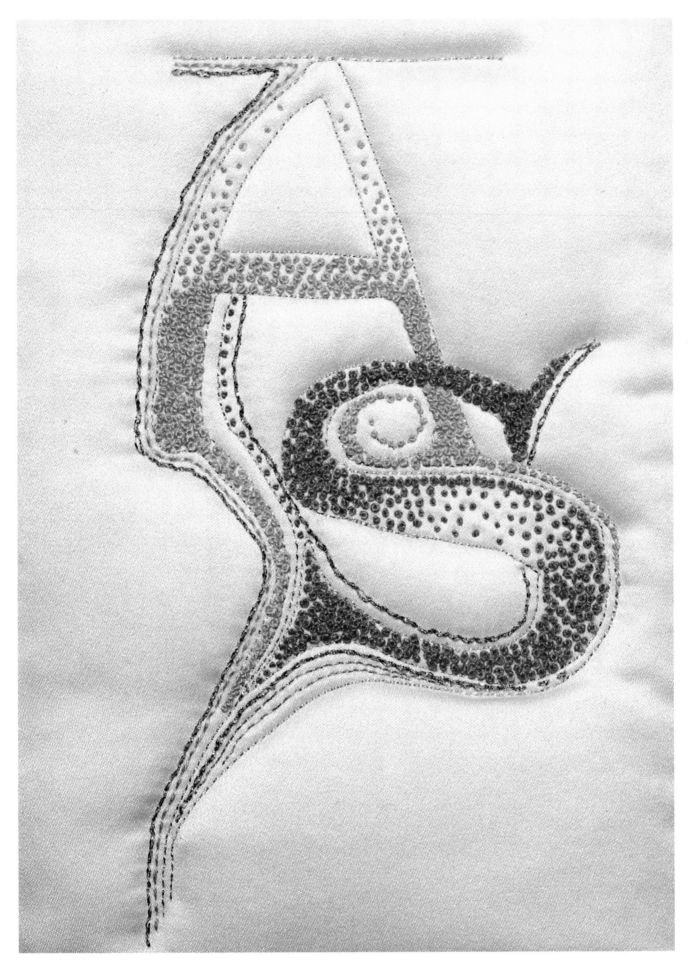

Ideas for lettering for the Church. By Pat Phillpott.

CHAPTER 6

Church Embroidery

by Jane Lemon

Designing for the Church – The 'Energy' frontal, Salisbury
Cathedral – Chasuble

Church Embroidery

Since the establishment of Christianity in this country, every generation has contributed to the building, decoration and care of our churches and cathedrals. This tradition continues today through our artists and musicians, poets and writers, craftsmen and embroiderers, who express through their work an active faith in the living church in the context of the twentieth century.

Designing for the Church

Design is all-important where embroidery is concerned. There is naturally a great deal of earlier work still in use, and because the general public has grown up with it it is considered by many parochial church councils to be the type of design best suited to their church, whatever the period in which it was built. What is often forgotten is that this embroidery was modern in its own time, and that work from our own period should be used in the same way.

Work for the church is not just a decoration but is an expression of belief, with the purpose of inspiring the congregation into wider and deeper thought. The design should be unique and personal to the proposed building with the theme arising from within; perhaps an architectural detail, a modern stained-glass window, the symbol of the saint to whom the church is dedicated, or some historic event of the locality. It is vital that the design combines with the whole interior setting, making a unified and satisfying visual whole.

The movement of line within the architecture and that within the embroidery must be in harmony. It is important to aim at this quality of movement and energy, especially in altar frontals in the larger churches and cathedrals, to draw the eye to the focal point. It is also helpful to the congregation if the design allows the eye to travel happily over it in a satisfying manner.

Although the design should read from the furthest point of a building, it must have the subtlety and technique to arouse momentum in interest as it is approached. This means that strength of line is needed, with plenty of supporting detail which can be savoured when closely examined.

Variation of tone is vital, a change of colour alone will not give the depth required to read from a distance. If the tone values of two important design areas do not vary sufficiently to show the line as the design requires, there are several methods that can be used to accentuate it. One of the areas may be padded and raised to create a shadow along the line, or the line may be strengthened by laying a darker handmade cord along the edge – this is not to recommend that shapes are outlined, but to help a design read from a distance – and it may not be noticeable until the frontal is viewed from the Sanctuary steps. If more strength is needed, then texturing is recommended on the unpadded section of the design, to build up the depth of the shadow. This can be done with machine stitching, running stitches, French knots or similar stitchery.

It is a temptation to have too much of a theatrical

Three-dimensional cross. *By Heidi Jenkins. Made of gold kid stretched over a base of cotton rope padded with felt. Beads provide the diagonal decorations.*

approach, and to assume that the view from a distance is all-important. This can result in the use of cheap fabrics and threads, and however good the design these do not do justice to a place of worship. With the rise in the cost of commissions and materials, the temptation is very understandable, but if the embroiders will stand by their convictions, the money is generally forthcoming when the difference in quality is explained. The finished results not only look far better, but will stand the test of time.

Colours must be selected in the building, and in the actual area where they will be used. The variations of light, and the result of the light being reflected off the stone, changes the colours appreciably – apart from the intensity of light being reduced. Very often, when the colour patterns are checked in the daylight, they appear too strong and garish, and one is tempted to substitute a quieter shade; but it is vital to stand by the decisions taken in the church, even if it means returning there to confirm one's choice.

The use of colour in the church is being more appreciated, as can be seen by the re-introduction of painted ceilings and organ pipes and the restoration of areas that originally were painted. Liturgical colours do have slight variations in their adoption, depending on which Cathedral Use is followed, but even these are being allowed a wider interpretation in order to suit the area or background that will incorporate the embroidery.

Consider the colour of the stone or brick when you select fabrics for vestments. Many a beautiful white, cream or pale yellow cope, or chasuble, disappears into the background when in use in the church. This applies especially to large buildings where the priest needs to be clearly visible from far back in the nave. For this reason too, care must be taken in selecting the pattern from which to cut the vestment, so that it fits the wearer and suits the environment.

Fabrics should be chosen to stand up to the wear and tear demanded of the article. A textural quality gives a lively start, but all depends on the overall design. It is vitally important to use good quality backing or inter-lining, not only to hold the embroidery but also to give substance and quality to the work. Choose metallised fabrics with great care, as some of them catch and snag

easily and a vestment incorporating them can look shoddy within a short space of time.

Fabrics selected for vestments should hang well and be thoroughly tested for creasing. Linen is very crush-able and difficult to look after in the vestry, whereas pure wool hangs out very quickly. Pure silk has a beauty and life of its own and is well worth the expense: it comes in so many weights and finishes that one can surely be found to fit every purpose, and the depth of colour is most rewarding.

Care must be taken with the choice of threads and techniques for vestments, as they must not be liable to catch on anything when folded or worn. See that the weight of the garment is well balanced, and not heavy or uncomfortable to wear.

The following pages show a recently designed frontal for Salisbury Cathedral, and a set of vestments for a village church. You can follow the progress of the frontal design from commission to making-up. The chasuble is a particularly good pattern that hangs well, and full instructions are given for making it up.

ALL SAINTS' CHURCH - STEEPLE LANGFORD)

Carved wooden motifs taken from the pulpit and Rector's stall - made from the original Jacobean 3 decker pulpit. dated 1613

Page from a designer's sketchbook. By Jane Lemon.

The 'Energy' Frontal, Salisbury Cathedral

The commission, given to Jane Lemon and the Sarum Group of the Embroiderers' Guild, was to design and make an all-seasons high altar frontal to link with the new east window, which was designed and made by Gabriel Loire, and unveiled and dedicated in May 1980.

The Sarum rite states that the frontal should be red, instead of the more usual green; but it was essential to use some blue to draw the window into the Sanctuary and to make it a visual whole with the altar.

The movement of colour in the design represents a living faith and the energy that is required to live as a practising Christian in the last quarter of the twentieth century.

The design of the chalice was taken from one recently discovered in a tomb under repair, and it was worked in Or Nué technique and leather. It is padded and stands away from the background by nearly 1in. (2.5cm.)

A great deal of research went into the various types of thorn, and a solid rose thorn was chosen instead of the needle-type blackthorn. This was because the great length of the nave required a very strong shape to read at the necessary distance.

The design was first presented to the Dean as a scale model cardboard cut-out 1in. = 1ft (2.5cm. = 30.5cm.)

'Energy' frontal from Salisbury Cathedral. *By Jane Lemon and members of the Sarum Group of the Embroiderers' Guild.* (Photograph by Sam Kelly, by permission of the Dean and Chapter).

to see if he approved of the general scheme and colouring. Having obtained the Dean's approval, the design was enlarged on to a good strong paper which formed the base on which coloured paper can be pinned and glued to make a full-size mock-up. This gives a very good impression for scale and tone, but, however near to the right colours the paper is, it will always be dead and flat compared to the actual fabric embroidery. The paper mock-up was then presented to the Dean and Chapter and was pinned up in position on the high altar for general review.

It takes a great deal of table or floor space to assemble the full-scale design. Space is also required for the frame on which the fabric is mounted, and it has been found that it is far more satisfactory to keep these large frontals on a permanent frame, which carries the weight and holds them taut, than to hang or roll them. When the work is finished, it can be stored without folding, and

Detail of 'Energy' frontal.

when in use it can be attached by Velcro to a throw-over cloth, made to fit the altar.

The permanent frame is mounted with linen or a good heavy calico using upholstery methods. Do not drive tacks home, or neaten the back, as the linen or calico will need to be re-tightened before the work is finally completed.

The chalice, and the crown of thorns divided into three sections, were worked separately on four slate frames and then applied to the permanent frame when the background was completed. The crown of thorns is worked in padded, manipulated and piped leathers of different colours and tones. The textural quality makes a strong contrast to the smoothness of the chalice.

To make the design read from a great distance when working in such a theatrical setting, it is often helpful to use a different technique for the appliqué, instead of the usual flat application. Each piece of fabric is cut with a 1in. (2.5cm.) turning, and bonded on to pelmet Vilene cut to the accurate shape. In some designs additional layers of felt may be tacked to the Vilene to give more height.

On the 'Energy' frontal the pale area behind the chalice was completely flat, then each following fabric shape was mounted on pelmet Vilene and lapped one on to another to give a progressively more raised effect towards the outside edges of the frontal. This meant that the turnings of the silk were turned back behind the Vilene on the inside edge of each swirl (and secured with herringbone stitch to give a clean, sharp finish) and the silk was left flat with a turning allowance on the Vilene of about 2½in. (6cm.) on the outside edge of the swirls. This allowed the next colour to be laid over the first and subsequently raised. Obviously the smaller pieces which lie completely on top of a single colour have to have the Vilene cut to shape and the turning of the silk herringboned back all the way round. The silk covered Vilene shapes are applied to the framed frontal with ladder stitch, using a curved needle where necessary.

This method gives a slight shadow on the edges of each colour, which gives depth and bite to the design. It also means that any machine or hand embroidery can

be worked on each prepared piece before it is applied to the frame.

Three members of the group worked on this particular frontal. Jane Lemon designed it and worked the crown of thorns. Mollie Collins worked the Or Nué chalice, and Catherine Talbot worked alongside Jane Lemon to cut out, construct and assemble the appliquéd background, and finally to apply the motives and cords.

It is possible to use as many embroiderers as the design allows, using separate frames. The Lenten frontal in Salisbury Cathedral had thirteen people working the pulled and drawn thread pieces. But it is essential to have one person to direct the work and to have the overall picture of the resulting embroidery, otherwise the result could be very unbalanced. It is possible to use up to four people sewing on the permanent frame if time is of the essence, but two or three is really more comfortable. Working together in a group is very stimulating, most supportive and above all rewarding and fun.

Chasuble

To make à pattern for this chasuble, scale up the graph on page 90 to make each square 1sq. in. (2.5sq. cm.), and cut out paper pattern pieces. Check that it will fit the wearer, and shorten or lengthen as required.

Make up the chasuble as follows:
1. Check fabric for direction of colour or nap.
2. Pin selvedges together.
3. Lay on pattern and pin in position.
4. Leave as a rectangular piece if embroidery is being worked.
5. Tack a line for centre back and centre front on fold of fabric.
6. Open up fabric and tack around the edge of the pattern to give shape, and to control cross-wise stretch or distortion when handling.
7. Frame-up on a calico backing if embroidery is being worked.
8. When the embroidery is completed, take the fabric off the frame and trim the calico back to the edge of the embroidery.
9. Cut out the back and front of the chasuble to shape, allowing 1in. (2.5cm.) all round, with 1½in. (4cm.) on the shoulder seams.
10. Lay the front and back pieces on to the interlining and cut out. The interlining can be tailors' canvas if there is a great weight of embroidery to carry; but if it is a light-coloured fabric, see that the dark tailors' canvas does not show through. Otherwise a fine calico, Vilene, stay-flex or organdie may be used.
11. Lock the fabric and interlining together with long catch stitches, making sure that the stitches do not show on the right side. Tack the two materials together on the fabric tack lines.
12. Cut out the lining with similar turnings.
13. Using the machine, flat-stitch the neck edge on the turning side of the tack line, and snip into the machine line at intervals.
14. Place the right side of the front of the chasuble to the right side of the back. Machine the shoulder seams together. Press.
15. Try the chasuble on the wearer to check that the head will go through the neck opening. If it is too small, extend the neck by opening up the shoulder. Do not lower the neck edge, as this will destroy the balance of the garment.

Chasuble. *By Jane Lemon. For St Mary's Church, Wylye, Wiltshire.*

16. Cut bias strips and cover enough narrow piping cord to go around the neck edge, and the hem edge if desired (piping cord should be boiled before use to prevent shrinkage).
17. There are two methods of applying piping:
(a) Machine it on to the tack line at the neck edge with the join on a shoulder seam; machine it on to the hem edge of the chasuble, on the tack line, with the join just back of a shoulder seam. The turnings are then turned over to the wrong side, and after cutting the turnings into layers to avoid bulk, they are catch-stitched on to the interlining and pressed on the wrong side.
(b) The neck edge and hem edge are turned over on the tack line, tacked, pressed and catch-stitched on to the interlining. The piping is then applied from the right side, by hand, with ladder stitch. The turnings are then layered and caught down on to the interlining.

Method (b) may take longer, but it gives a beautiful finish with no tension problems. If the fabric is a velvet or thick tweed, a toning silk piping makes a most attractive finish.
18. The shoulder seams of the lining can now be machined with any alterations that were made at the fitting. Catch-stitch the shoulder turning of the chasuble to the shoulder turning of the lining, so that the shoulder seams lie on top of one another.
19. With the chasuble inside out, lay the lining flat and catch-stitch it from the wrong side to the interlining in a couple of places, to prevent it ballooning.
20. Lay the lining flat to the edge, and without tightening the lining turn the seam allowance under, and lay the folded edge to meet the piping. Pin in position.
21. Try the chasuble on someone to check that the lining is not anywhere pulling the main fabric.
22. Ladder-stitch the lining to the machine line of the piping with small stitches. Press the fold, taking the edge of the iron up to the piping, but not on to it.

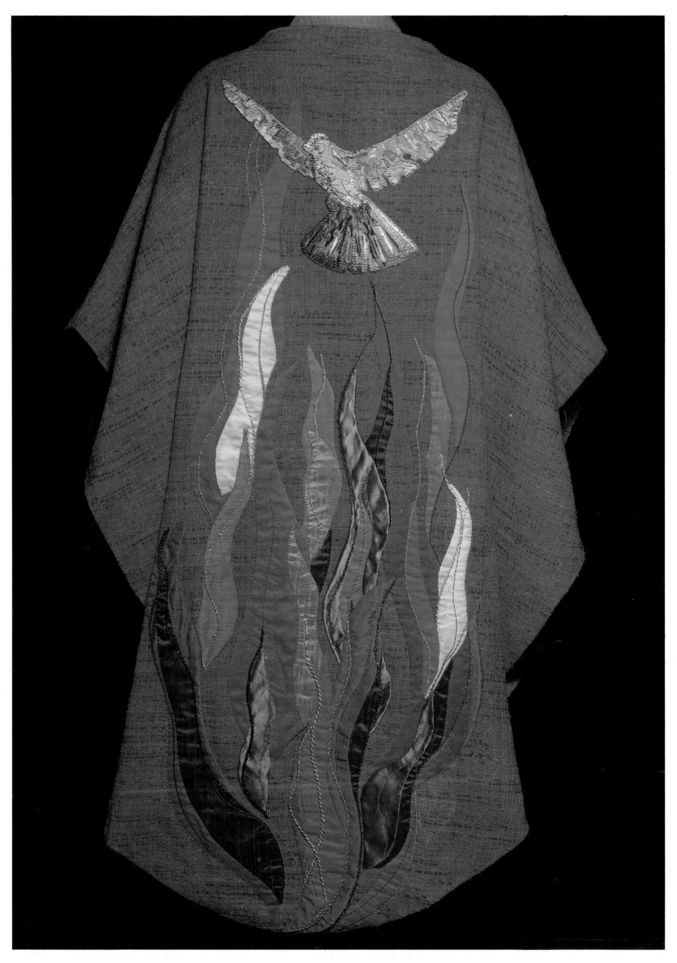

Detail from the chasuble (see page 89).

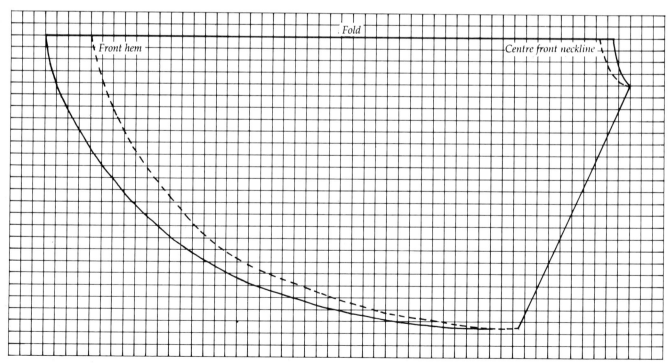

Fold

Front hem

Centre front neckline

Pattern for the chasuble, scale 2.5cm. to a square. By Jane Lemon.

Set of burse, veil and stole matching the chasuble. By Jane Lemon. Also for St Mary's Church, Wylye.

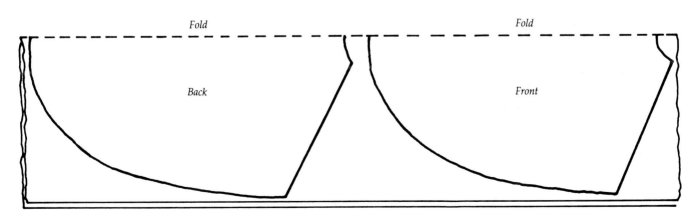

Cutting layout for chasuble.

Burse. *By Heidi Jenkins. Metal-thread embroidery on green shot silk.*

The four designs in the centre show traditional goldwork techniques on four different cross designs:
1. Raised shape covered with couching in New Jap gold.
2. Cut lengths of bright purl and check purl with bead centre.
3. Check purl and New Jap gold couched with green sewing silk.
4. Or nué technique in two tones of green.

Some of the outer squares make use of sequin waste, gold plate bands, brass washers, beads, pearls and purl grit (tiny pieces of purl). Others are filled with needle-lace stitches using a variety of metal threads.

CHAPTER 7

Beadwork

by Jane Dew and Valerie Campbell-Harding

Types of beads and sequins – Equipment – Fabrics – Design – Colour – Framing-up – Transferring the design – Ways of attaching beads – Tambour beading – Sequins – Jewels, glass and stones

Beadwork

by Jane Dew

Beadwork has an affinity with goldwork. The reason is, the thread attaches an object (purls or a bead) to the fabric rather than forming a stitch, and the reflection of light is a characteristic of both methods.

The word bead means 'a prayer', and originated from little balls strung together for counting prayers such as the present-day Rosary. The word now covers beads of all sizes and shapes which are used for jewellery, embroidery and fashion and for religious and ceremonial occasions.

Beads for embroidery come in a great variety of shapes and sizes and in myriad different materials, colours, and textures – the types listed below are those most commonly used:

TYPES OF BEADS AND SEQUINS

The smallest beads are little larger than a pinhead. In this category come faceted beads known as cut beads, as well as pearls and rocaille. A variety of colours and textures can be obtained: matt, metallic, mother-of-pearl (MOP), clear, iridescent (iris), and silver-lined (which are clear glass with a silver lined thread hole).

Long beads are called bugles, and vary in length from fractions of an inch to 6in. (15cm.)

Flat sequins (the name is derived from an old Italian coin called a zecchino) are circles of plastic with a central hole, and are available in matt, MOP, iris and metallic form. In the past sequins were made of metal and known as 'spangles'. Home-made sequins can be made with a leather punch.

Cup sequins are domed instead of flat.

Paillettes (so named from the equipment of enamellers) are sequins in oval, flower, feather and leaf shapes with one or more holes.

Miscellaneous beads include droppers, faceted and metallic beads, those in cut-glass and wood as well as jewellery stones, the range varying according to the stockist.

EQUIPMENT

Beadwork is a fine technique involving components which, individually, have a life of their own, and which when massed can be quite heavy. The equipment and framing-up therefore reflect this dual role.

Frame

All beadwork should be carried out on a frame, thus keeping the fabric at the correct tension to support the work and, at the same time, leaving both hands free. A standing ring frame, or a table clamp tambour frame would be ideal for a small piece of work. If the outer ring is kept slightly proud of the surface of the fabric, then spare beads placed on the embroidery will not run off and be lost. Larger pieces should be mounted in a slate frame.

Thimble

A thimble is essential for the accurate placing of the needle, and protects the middle finger when an especially fine beading needle is being used.

Scissors

Small sharp-pointed embroidery scissors.

Tweezers

These are ideal for picking up beads.

Needles

Beading needles are long and very fine (they are sometimes known as 'straw' needles). They slip through the centre of even the tiniest beads, and they enable easier selection of particular beads. 'Betweens' are a reasonable substitute, but their shorter length makes them a little cumbersome.

Beading pad

This is a small piece of stout cardboard, sometimes lightly padded and covered in felt or velvet, which is used to hold a selection of beads whilst working.

Containers

Always make careful arrangements for storing beads. Whilst they provide delight in their correct place on fabric, they can be infuriating when let loose, and at some time in the processes of beadwork a container is bound to be dropped on the floor. Limit this possibility by separating types and colours of bead, and keeping small numbers in polythene envelopes that are securely closed, which in turn can be stored in small jars or plastic boxes. Use clear containers so that beads can be chosen without having to open each package.

Sewing threads

Use a strong sewing thread which can be beeswaxed if necessary. Nylon 'invisible' thread may be found to be unwieldy, and machine embroidery threads are too thin. Use a colour which tones either with the background fabric or the overall colour of the beads.

Beadwork in progress. *By Dorothy Reglar. A section of beadwork on organdie, part of a fashion project. The design is lightly marked out and the beads are sewn on to fill the spaces in a regular manner.*

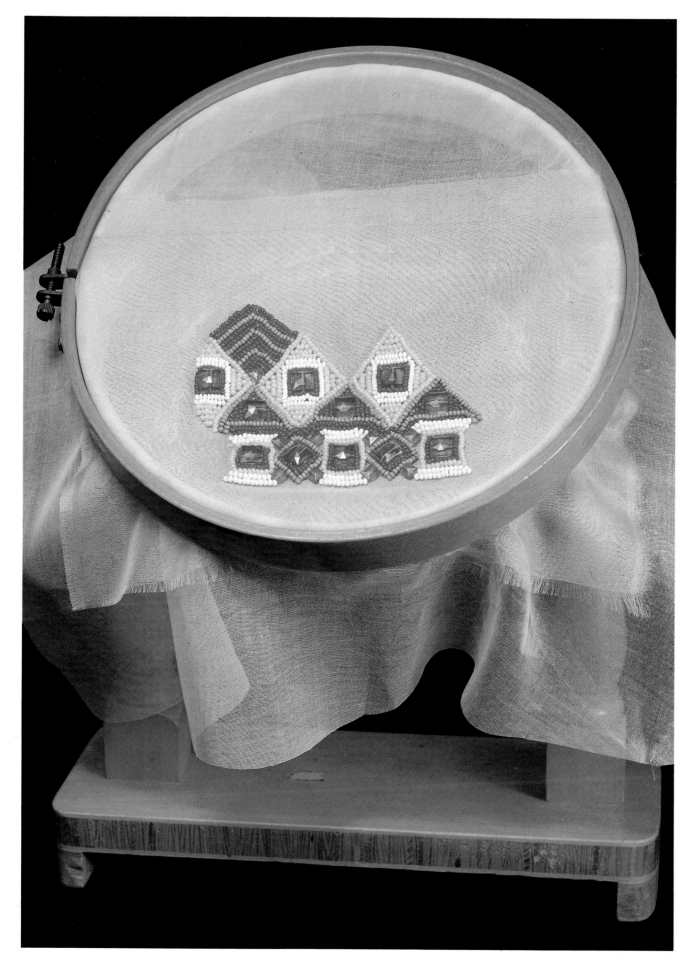

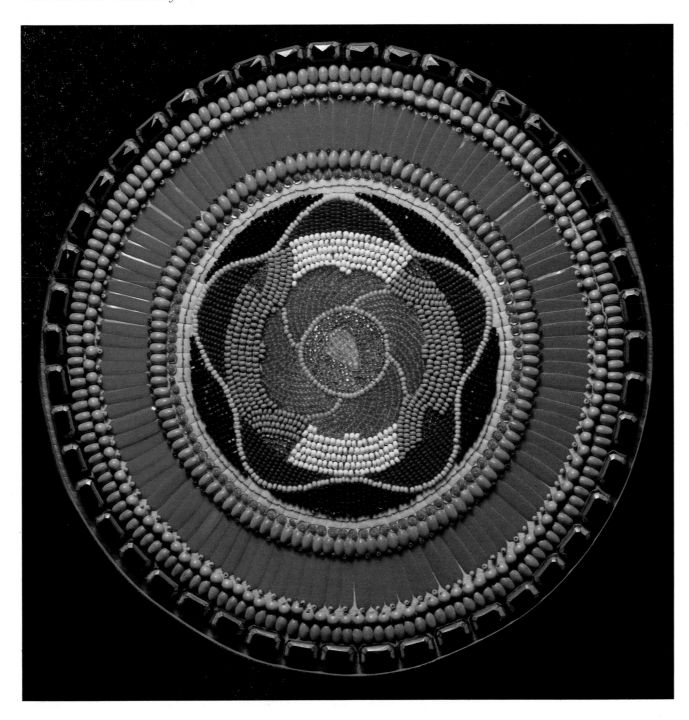

Circular beadwork panel. *By Dorothy Reglar. A design consisting entirely of beads of various kinds, mounted in a black perspex frame.*

FABRICS

Ideally the fabric should reflect the character of beadwork, and so should complement the type of bead chosen, and the end-use of the work. The fabric must be capable of supporting the weight of the beads, so that light and fine fabrics will require a backing. Plain fabrics will show off a design well, and printed or woven patterns can be developed and accentuated by beadwork.

DESIGN

Beads reflect light, so that designs that have changes in direction allow light to strike the beads from different angles. In dress embroidery there is the added interest of a moving three-dimensional body.

Designs that flow will give the embroiderer scope to explore beadwork to its fullest potential. Sources for flowing designs can be found in photographs of rock formations, tree bark, river beds, seashores at low tide, contour lines on maps, etc. A simple way to achieve a flowing design is to drop a soft cord on to the framed fabric and catch it down where it lies, thus giving an instant basis for a design.

As you gain in confidence, you can tackle designs that require more accuracy, using sources that have a more geometric quality such as architecture. Experimental work can be tried on unusual fabrics like PVC, and on present-day interpretations of bead canvas work, which was so popular in the nineteenth century.

If a specific use is envisaged for a piece of work, consider the scale of the article and its use before embarking on the design and choosing the materials. The 'precious' quality of beadwork tends to direct its use towards boxes, bags, belts and dress embroidery; but it can also be used with advantage on book covers, panels and three-dimensional soft sculpture.

Ideas may develop from a particular piece of fabric or a wonderful 'find' in a haberdashery department, bead shop or jumble sale – and the use for that piece of work can be decided on completion, if materials and techniques 'marry' successfully and if careful preparations are made to ensure that the design is well placed on a spacious background.

COLOUR

Too many colours detract from the texture, and emphasis is better achieved with different sizes of bead, density of texture and changes in character – for example, shiny against matt, opaque against transparent, bead against sequin. Large and shiny beads and sequins are more dominant than small and matt ones, but massed matt beads can balance small shiny ones.

A scheme which is fairly assured of success is to use beads in shades of one colour.

FRAMING-UP

Always use a frame large enough for the work, a ring frame for small pieces, and a slate or home-made frame for larger pieces. Instructions for framing up are on pages 20 and 22.

If the fabric is light, first mount up the backing, which may be fine sheeting, lawn, organdie or calico.

TRANSFERRING THE DESIGN

Use any of the methods on pages 42–3 which are suitable for the design and the fabric.

Technique

1. Select a few of the required beads and place them on the beading pad near the working hand. Cut a short length of thread, about 12in. (30cm.) as work tends to fray a longer length. Run the thread through beeswax if the work is to be worn or used. Choose a beading needle to suit the selected beads, thread up, and a firm knot and a small catch stitch at the back gives the work a secure start. Finish off in the same way. Select the beads with the needle, picking them up and letting them slide down on to the fabric before securing them with a small stitch. The placing of beads and sequins improves with practice as one can assess the place for the next stitch.
2. Beads can be used in formal patterns or disposed within an area. They can be used to create shadows and highlights, or to achieve textures of varying density. A single one can be nestled inside a sequin or used to hold

a larger bead. Beads need not only be attached singly, they can also be applied one above the other in piles, laid in curled strings, or tumbled about in heaps.
3. Small back stitch for a continuous line of beads.
4. Larger back stitch for groups of beads. (Always use odd numbers.)
5. Small running stitch for sequins and beads.
6. Back stitch for a continuous line of sequins.
7. Zigzag stitching for line of parallel bugle beads.
8. Large back stitch for line of end to end bugle beads.

WAYS OF ATTACHING BEADS

See below
1. Beads can be secured by a single stitch through the hole.
2. A tiny bead in the centre of a large one stops the thread pulling through.
3. A pile of small beads can be anchored with three threads through the centre spaced round the pile.
4. To make short hanging lengths of beads, take a stitch through the final one and then pass the needle back again through the others.

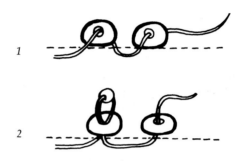

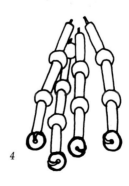

Tambour beading

This is a quick method of attaching beads to fabric using a tambour frame and hook. These are generally employed by professional workshops where there is a lot of beading to be done on garments.

The tambour frame is shaped like a drum, and consists of two wooden rings fitting closely together between which the fabric is stretched, in much the same way as a ring frame is used for embroidery. Tambour frames always have a stand, or are clamped to a table. The hook resembles a very fine metal crochet hook.

Designs for tambouring are based on a continuous line. The beads or sequins are supplied strung on a thread, which is secured to the right side of the framed fabric. The design is marked on the wrong side, which is uppermost in the frame. The hook pierces the fabric, picks up a loop of thread between two beads and brings it back up to the top side, goes down again a bead-length ahead on the line and picks up another loop, leaving the previous loop lying on the wrong side, and the result is a row of beads on the right side and a row of chain stitches on the wrong side. This method relies on perfect tension for the loops and accurate matching of the length of the loops on the wrong side to the length of the beads on the right side.

Beadwork panel. *By Jane Dew. A close-up of part of a panel consisting of a mass of brilliantly coloured beads of different shapes and sizes.*

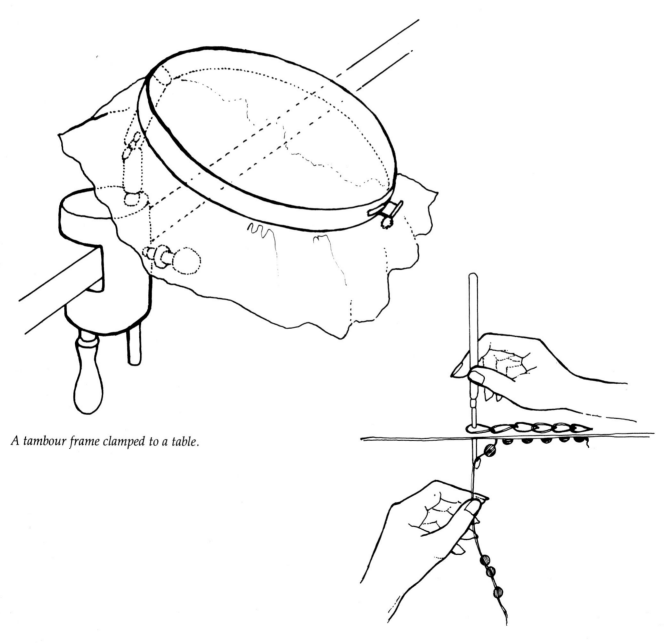

A tambour frame clamped to a table.

The technique of tambouring.

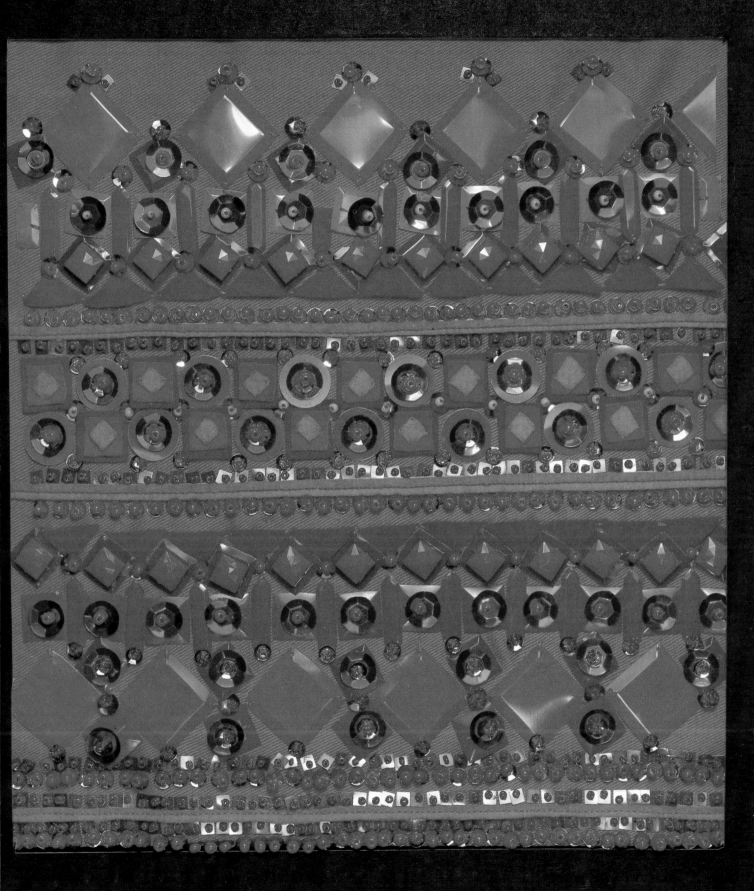

Sequins

by Valerie Campbell-Harding

There are innumerable ways of using sequins: they can form a line or fill an area; they can accentuate a pattern or form a highlight; or they can be used on their own as a shape in their own right. As they are generally so much brighter and more reflective than most beads, they need to be used with care so that they do not dominate the design.

As sequins present more of a surface for decorative stitchery than do beads, there is more scope for attaching them in interesting ways:

1. Each sequin is attached with a back stitch, which is then covered with the next sequin.
2. Single stitches each side are made through lengths of cut purl.
3. Four chain stitches can be worked in a pattern over the top of each sequin.
4. Four lengths of cut purl will form a square, securing four sequins.
5. Sequins held by central beads and knots.
6. Sequins held by stitchery.

1

2

3

4

5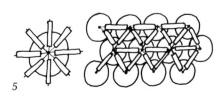

Butterfly design: *different treatments. By Edwina Stacey. Top. The wings are entirely filled with beads and sequins, and the body consists of tiny beads.*

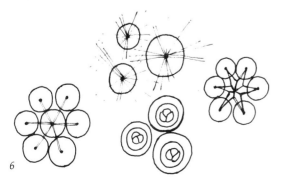

6

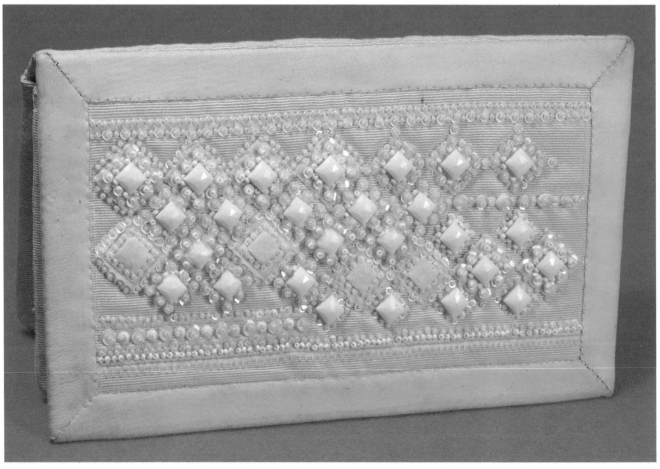

Opposite, above. **Butterfly design.** *By Edwina Stacey.*
The wings are outlined in long and short stitch in two shades of
blue, and a few sequins are used as highlights.

Lilac blossom. *By Mavis Graham. A spray of lilac*
embroidered in gold bugle beads, crystal and gold beads,
sequins and pearls, with a little added stitchery.

Opposite, below. **Beaded evening bag.** *By Jane Dew.*
Beadwork on ribbed silk framed in fine suede.

On these pages the metallic glitter of sequins is used
in several ways – as points of light on the edge of a butterfly's wing, in massed form as tiny flowerheads, and
as part of a formal pattern on an evening bag.

Overleaf, punched sequins form part of a repeated
eyelet pattern, and sequin waste (perforated sheet
sequin) makes a rich background to raised motifs in
leather and bugle beads.

Like all eye-catching material, sequins should be
used with a purposeful idea of their contribution to the
final effect, and their reflective light should blend into
the design as a whole.

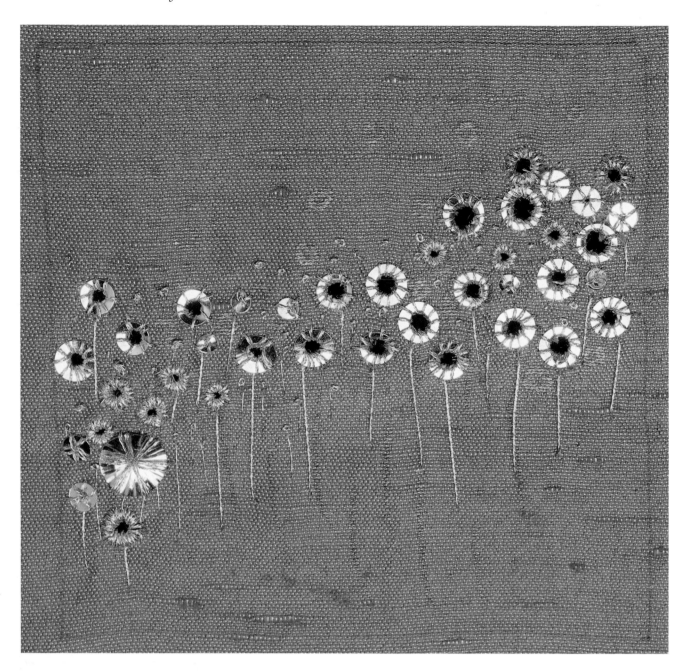

Sequin flowers. *By Vera Dawson. A miniature flower garden worked in* broderie anglaise *technique with gold thread and punched-out sequins. The background is lightly painted.*

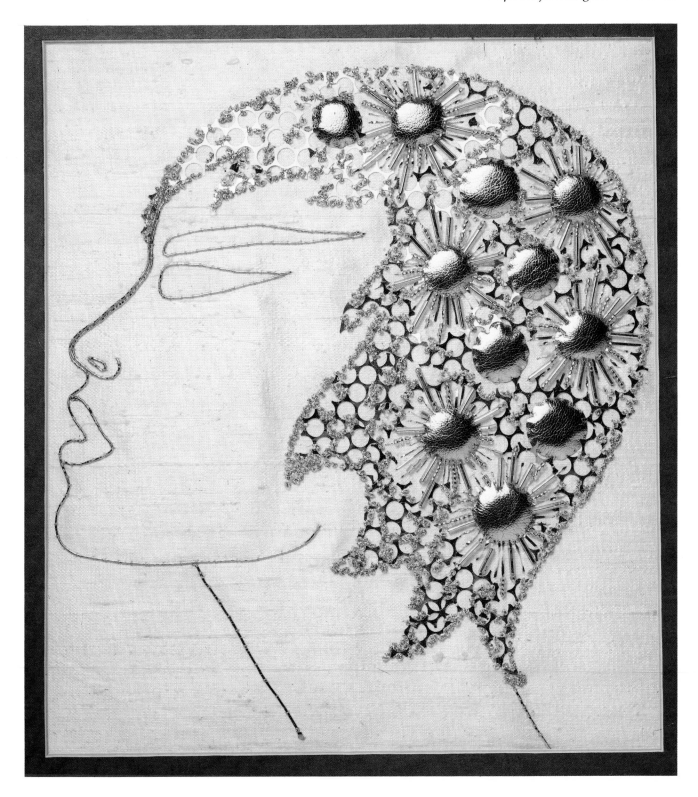

Head in free goldwork. *By Lyn Hughes. Worked on a slub silk background, the profile is in couched Jap gold. The cap is worked in padded gold kid and beadwork set in sequin waste, which is held down with French knots in gold crochet thread.*

Jewels, glass, and stones

'Jewels' in embroidery, generally are cut faceted pieces of coloured glass, with one or more holes pierced near the edge to secure them to the fabric. Jewels are often attached in decorative ways, with surrounding stitchery to conceal the stitches through the holes.

1. Basic method of attaching a jewel, with stitches through the holes.

2. The stitches through the holes are threaded with cut purl, and the jewel is edged with tiny beads.

3.–6. Jewels held in place with stitches through the holes, and then surrounded with cut purl or metal threads.

Polished stones are often used with metal-thread embroidery, and also other objects such as shavings of mother-of-pearl, shells, coins, lumps of glass, pebbles and slices of wood, none of which have holes for stitching. These can be attached by adhesive, by covering the object with a net of stitchery such as needle-weaving, or by embedding them in leather or non-woven fabric.

Goldwork panel. *By Kit Pyman. A design based upon microphotographs of muscle fibres. The Italian quilting in the background was worked on the machine with a twin needle, and the embroidery includes couched gold threads, applied leather, cut purl and beads. The oval polished stone had no holes, and is held in place with glue, a net of nylon thread and a tight band of gold wire around the base.*

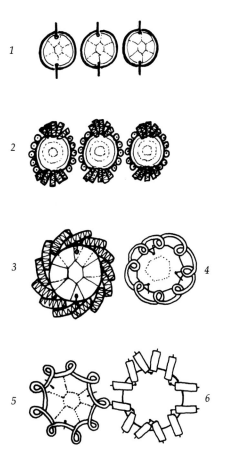

Ideas for securing jewels and stones.

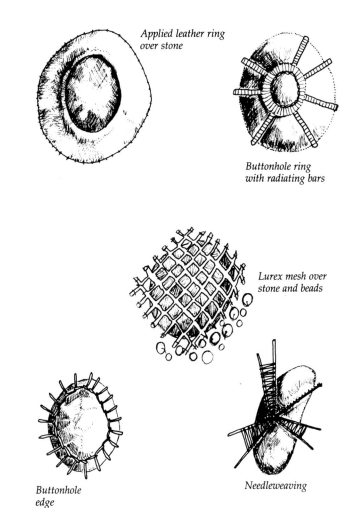

Applied leather ring over stone

Buttonhole ring with radiating bars

Lurex mesh over stone and beads

Buttonhole edge

Needleweaving

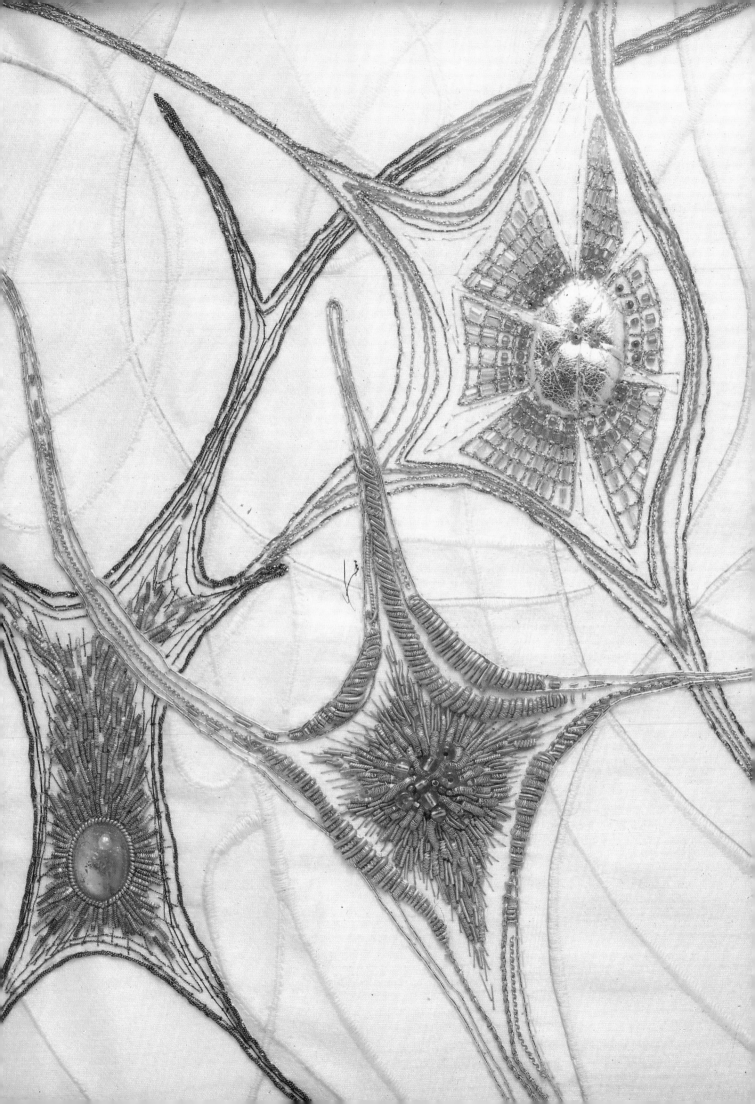

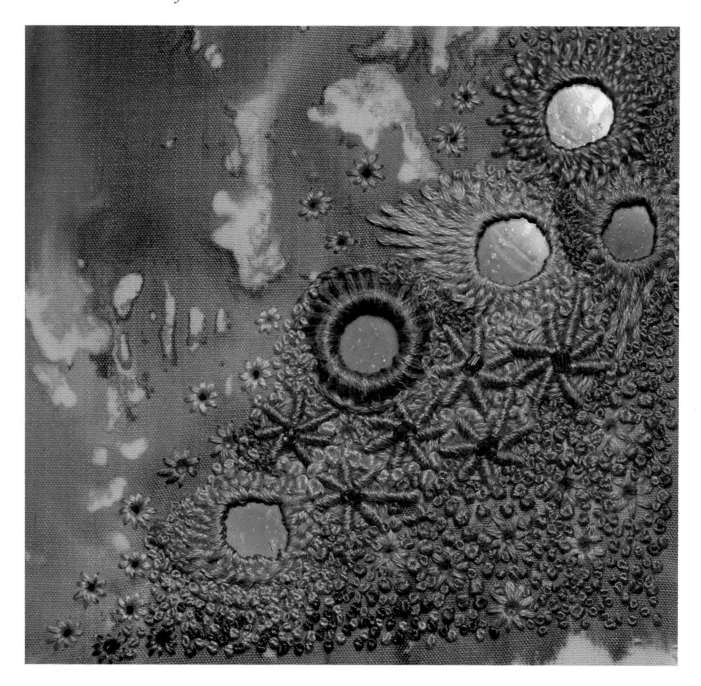

Shisha glass

Shisha, or mirror glass, is mica of a silvery grey colour with small imperfections on the surface. There are no holes to sew through, but the pieces can be held under net or transparent fabric, or can have stitching over the top. Pieces of shisha come in small, irregular shapes, and add shine to embroidery.

One of the stitchery methods of attachment is as follows:

Make four straight stitches over the glass. On the second round make a knot at each corner to secure the stitches. On this foundation, Cretan stitch (or other stitches such as buttonhole) can be worked solidly around the edge.

Shisha with dyeing and hand embroidery. *By Peggy Northen. Waterproof inks sprayed on to a damp cotton background forms the basis of this design. Shisha glass was attached with Cretan stitch, and the embroidery was built up with wheels, eyelets, beads and myriad French knots.*

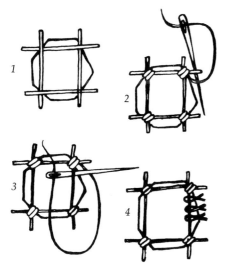

Shisha with metallic thread. *By Celia Stanley. A design of firework explosions embroidered by machine on a green slub silk with multi-coloured thread. The shisha was applied by hand in the usual way using the same metallic threads.*

Goldwork sample with various materials. *By Vera Dawson. A design based on circles using Jap gold, sequins, shisha glass and dyed plastic tubing.*

Embroidered panel, centred with shisha. *By Kathryn Biggam. A layered embroidery on silk, with couching and laidwork and applied leather, centred with shisha glass which emphasizes the perspective.*

Index

'Anenomes' 46
Appliqué 41ff
Appliqué techniques – detached 50
    hand 44
    machine 46
Appliqué – transferring designs 42

'Battle Array' 43
Beadwork 93ff.
Beadwork in progress 95
Beadwork panel 99
Bed 11
Beeswax 18
'Beetle' panel 23
Belt – machine embroidered 67
    gold-beaded 9
Book cover 25
Box – 'Sea-chest' 9
    Circular 73
Braid 29
Buckle 40
Bullion 8
Burse 92
Burse, veil and stole 91
Butterfly – sample – sequinned 100
    sample – embroidered 102
Buttons in Or nué 32

Canvas-work with metal threads 34
Card – for padding 24
Chair back – PVC 44
Chasuble – pattern 90
Church embroidery 83ff.
Circular beadwork pattern 96
Circular panel in couched gold 29
Cords 29
Couching – machine 58
    metal threads 26
Cross – three-dimensional 84
Cushion – machine appliqué 55
    machine embroidery 59
    machine patchwork 65
Cutting board 18

Designs – to transfer 42
Drawstring bag with purls 37

Evening bag – beaded 102
    machine embroidered print 63
    machine embroidered 60
Evening sweater 51

Face cloth 48
Felt – for padding 22
Field of Cloth of Gold 11
Flower, detached 50
Flower panel in detached appliqué 49
Frames and framing-up – for Beadwork 95
    home-made 20
    ring 22
    slate 20
    tambour 98
Frame for an ikon photograph 34
Frontal (altar) 86
Fungi – quilted panels and designs 38–9

Glass 106
Goldwork panel 107
Goldwork sample 110

Handkerchiefs – machine embroidered 72
Head in free goldwork 105
Hems – machined 70

Jewels 106

Laidwork with metal threads 12
Leather 22
Letter 'S' 78
Lettering 75ff.
Lilac blossom 103
Log Cabin patchwork method 66

Machine – to choose 54
Machine appliqué 46ff.
Machine embroidery – 53ff.
Mediaeval tents 10
Metal threads 17
Metal-thread work – development, use 16
    history 8
    techniques 26
Monogram 'A.S.' 81
Monograms 79

Or nué 31
Opus Anglicanum 10

Padding 22
Patchwork cushion 65
Plate 29
Pole screen 'Scabious' 52
Pulled thread work with metal thread 13
Purls 35

Quilting along the seam 65
Quilting – trapunto 24

Russia braid 29

St Cuthbert's maniple 10
Sequin flowers 104
Sequins – use of 100
Shisha centred panel 111
Shisha with metallic thread 109
Shisha with painting 108
Spool cases 60
Stones 106
String – for padding 30

Table mats 68
Table napkins 70
Tambour beading 98
'The Shape of Israel' 12
Towel with applied flower 48
Transferring designs 42

Underside couching 10

Waistcoat – PVC 45
    silk with applied leather 24
Work in progress 'Calyx' 21

Useful addresses

THE EMBROIDERERS' GUILD is for those interested in all types of embroidery. Facilities include classes, workshops, exhibitions, a large reference library and a unique collection of historical embroidery. Membership is open to all. Send SAE for details to The Secretary, The Embroiderers' Guild, Apartment 41A, Hampton Court Palace, East Molesey, Surrey KT8 9AU.

THE ROYAL SCHOOL OF NEEDLEWORK runs day and evening classes and a two-year certificate course. Embroidery supplies are available on the premises and by mail order. Apply to The Secretary, The Royal School of Needlework, 25 Princes Gate, London SW7 1QE.

THE EMBROIDERERS' GUILD OF AMERICA,
200 Fourth Avenue, Louisville, Kentucky 40202, U.S.A.

THE EMBROIDERERS' GUILD OF AUSTRALIA,
175 Elizabeth Street, Sydney, New South Wales 2000, Australia.

THE EMBROIDERERS' GUILD OF VICTORIA,
170 Wattletree Road, Malvern, Victoria 3144, Australia.

ASSOCIATION OF N.Z. EMBROIDERERS' GUILD,
171 The Ridgeway, Mornington, Wellington 2, New Zealand.

CANADIAN EMBROIDERERS' GUILD,
PO Box 541, Station B, London, Ontario N6A 4W1, Canada.